DESIGN UK

DESIGN UK MAX FRASER

First published in 2001 by
Conran Octopus Limited
a part of Octopus Publishing Group
2–4 Heron Quays, London E14 4JP
Visit our website at www.conran-octopus.co.uk

Reprinted in 2002

To order please ring Conran Octopus Direct
on 01933 443863

Text copyright © 2001 Max Fraser
Book design and layout copyright
© 2001 Conran Octopus Limited
With the support of Mazda Cars UK

British Library Cataloguing-in-Publication Data.
A catalogue record for this book is available
from the British Library.

ISBN: 1 84091 198 0

Publishing Director: Lorraine Dickey
Commissioning Editor: Bridget Hopkinson
Copy Editor: Robert Anderson
Creative Director: Leslie Harrington
Design: johnson banks
Picture Research: Clare Limpus
Production Director: Zoe Fawcett
Production: Alex Wiltshire

Printed in Europe

conran
OCTOPUS

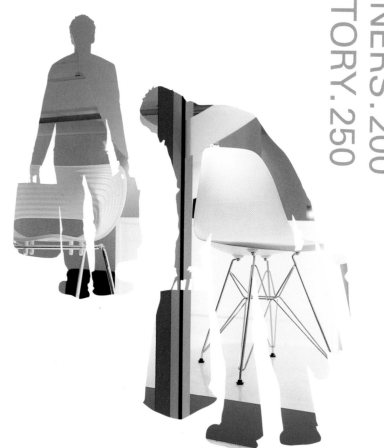

INTRODUCTION

The start of the new millennium is here. The global Information Age is upon us and technology is moving faster than ever before. The human race is the most productive it has ever been and consequently we work longer and harder to keep up with the technologies we have created. Free time is at a premium and 'stress' has become a buzzword – the act of working to one's absolute limits now somewhat de rigeur.

Constantly bombarded with slogans and brand names, we crave the things that remind us that we are individuals, not brainwashed corporate targets. Our homes have become sanctuaries, places where we are truly able to define our identities and express our own unique personalities through the objects that we put in them. And the quality of these objects can add a whole extra dimension to our living environments – there is nothing quite like a well-designed piece of furniture crafted with exceptional production values or a sculptural light that you will not find in anyone else's home. The perfect marriage of form and function not only helps our lives to run more efficiently, but introduces that special 'x factor' to our interior spaces, an aesthetic, almost spiritual element that is so often lacking in the outside world. It was this realization that first attracted me to product design. My interest took me to New York City, a cultural hot spot that I had always wished to explore. I wanted to discover the city's approach to design retailing and I set out to scour the streets of Manhattan in search of its meccas of 'design cool'. After a few days, reality set in. I really was an Englishman in New York and my frustration at not being able to penetrate the NYC design scene grew. I found it peculiar that amidst the plethora of guide books to this most style-conscious of cities, there wasn't one that targeted the 'where it's at' in contemporary design. It was then that the idea for *Design UK* was born as I realized that, indeed, the UK was lacking a guide to its own design world.

The UK is internationally recognized as a hotbed of creative talent, its influences spanning the globe. But the design scene, despite its growing accessibility via the press, is still seen by many as an elitist environment reserved only for the wealthy and those in the know. Although this perception holds an element of truth, the aim of this book is to dispel this attitude by simply presenting the scene as it is – out there and open to all of us.

Design UK is intended to attract both the trade professional and the design-conscious consumer. For this book is as much about shopping as it is about design. It will tell you where to find the latest in lighting, the quirkiest retro ceramics and the coolest sofas. The shops in this book, drawn from across the country, cover a huge cross-section of products that will appeal to everyone interested in contemporary design. Accompanied by reviews and tantalizing photographs, I hope you will feel encouraged to go out and explore these innovative retail outlets. The designer section profiles a selection of newly established furniture, lighting and accessory designers who have managed to withstand the difficulties of UK manufacturing to produce fantastically innovative and beautiful interior objects – prepare to be inspired.

The world of furniture and product design is certainly an exciting place. Use this book to discover this world for yourself and should you uncover any more hidden gems on your journeys, please let me know.

Max Fraser
designuk@maxfraser.com

Icons
These icons will enable you to see at a glance which products are stocked in each store and the specialist areas of each designer.

 originals

 furniture

 lighting

 glassware & ceramics

 textiles

 tableware

 jewellery

 clothing

ALMA HOME CHAPLINS OF L
DOMUS KUME MAC DOMAI
DE LA ESPADA AIMÉ BOWWO
MINT FUNCTION GRAHAM &
RETRO HOME OVERDOSE ON
DESIGNERS GUILD LUNA ATO
ENGLAND AT HOME INTOVIE
LIVING SPACE NOEL HENNE
PURVES & PURVES UTILITY (
KATE WIGGIN PURE LIVING
CHRISTOPHER FARR MASON
HARRODS – THE CONTEMPOR
PLACES AND SPACES CHARL

NDON LIPP INTERIOR DESIGN
INTERIORS BOOM! MAKERS
THE CONRAN SHOP HABITAT
REEN BOWLES AND LINARES
ESIGN NIGEL COATES PREGO
IC ISOKON PLUS SHOPS SCP
PLANET BAZAAR SKANDIUM
Y FURNITURE MUJI VIADUCT
OFFREY DRAYTON SUBURBIA
OYD DAVIES CENTRAL FLOW
OP UK TWENTYTWENTYONE
Y GALLERY OGIER THE CUBE
PAGE FANDANGO TOM TOM

ACADIA

DESIGNERS INCLUDE:
Marcel Breuer
Le Corbusier
Paul Dean
Charles and Ray Eames
Catherine Hough
Jasper Morrison
Giulietta del Signore

Acadia
11–13 Essex Road
London N1 2SE
020 7354 4464
www.acadiauk.com
Tube: Angel
Open: Mon–Sat 10–7 (closed Tues)
Sun 1–6

Acadia originally opened in Clerkenwell
in 1997, but two years later moved to
larger, more suitable premises, where it
now displays a wide selection of furniture,
lighting and accessories for the home
and office. Acadia is a valuable resource
for any lover of furniture and design,
offering a mix of high-quality pieces
from both established and up-and-coming
designers. Furniture by Le Corbusier,
Breuer and Eames sits comfortably
alongside contemporary works by talented
new designers, such as glassware by
Catherine Hough, hand-printed textiles
by Giulietta del Signore, and functional
understated furniture by Paul Dean.

Dean is Acadia's resident designer and
maker. His handsome collection
comprises bookshelves and side, coffee
and dining tables, and many of the pieces
combine beautiful hardwoods with
stainless steel or aluminium. And because
Acadia's sister company, Pearl Dot Ltd,
is responsible for manufacturing Dean's
work, each piece can be tailor-made to suit
your requirements.

Whether you are buying or just
browsing, Acadia's staff are helpful,
friendly and unintimidating, making a visit
to their shop a worthwhile pleasure.

AERO

Aero
96 Westbourne Grove
London W2 5RT
020 7221 1950
shop1@aero-furniture.com
Tube: Notting Hill Gate
Open: Mon – Sat 10 – 6:30
Sun 12 – 5

347–349 King's Road
London SW3 5ES
020 7351 0511
Tube: Sloane Square,
then bus along the King's Road
Open: Mon – Sat 10 – 6:30
Sun 12 – 5

Aero's original premises on Westbourne Grove opened about 12 years ago as one of the area's first contemporary design shops. Showcasing an array of both classic and cutting-edge furniture, lighting and accessories to a diverse clientele, Aero has helped facilitate the growth of public interest in modern design over recent years. In 1998 the shop's popularity prompted the launch of a second shop on Chelsea's King's Road, to attract the wealthy and increasingly open-minded residents of SW3. More recently Aero has had a facelift with both stores renovated and given a fresher and sharper image.

All the same, Aero does not necessarily charge the high prices you might expect. Pieces from classic names such as Jacobsen, Eames, Le Corbusier, Panton and Gray will always be fairly pricey, but there are plenty of offerings here to please those with more modest budgets. On the ground floor of the Westbourne Grove branch there are affordable accessories, such as Stelton and Zack stainless-steel cutlery, iittala and LSA International glassware, ASA ceramics, Global knives and Authentic's range of 'plastic fantastics', while in the basement can be found most of the store's stock of furniture and lighting. Both style and price vary massively, simply because Aero is trying to appeal to as broad a clientele as possible. During my own visits to Aero I found the staff a little complacent, but since the renovation, the attitudes and ambience are certainly more up beat. Nevertheless, it is well worth deciding for yourself whether Aero still merits its place as a populist pioneer in the current wave of interest in contemporary design.

DESIGNERS INCLUDE:
ASA
Authentic
Le Corbusier
Charles and Ray Eames
Global
Eileen Gray
iittala
Arne Jacobsen
LSA International
Verner Panton
Stelton
Zack

Aero
new angles on living

Aimé
32 Ledbury Road
London W11 2AB
020 7221 7070
Tube: Notting Hill Gate
Open: Mon – Sat 10:30 – 7

In March 1999 Parisian sisters Val and Vanda Heng Vong opened Aimé on London's fashionable Ledbury Road. In an attempt to break free from the traditional image of French design generally plied in the British capital – all Louis-Quinze finery and fairy-tale châteaux – they decided to specialize in French products with a distinctly contemporary feel. The result is an elegant shop on two floors, combining women's fashion with glass and ceramic tableware and accessories, as well as a small choice of furniture, lighting, linen and artwork. Everything is well displayed in the shop's light and airy space, its colour scheme of white, grey and cream enlivened by the splashes of colour provided by the products themselves.

Aimé's offerings can be surprisingly affordable – simple hand-blown tumblers by Henry Dean are a must-have at only £3 each – but price always comes second in consideration to the quality and interest of particular pieces, allowing room for both the modular ceramic tableware of Carine Tontini and the 'contemporary rustic' feel of plates by the long-established company Molin. Slick lighting by young designer Christophe Delcourt (pictured) deserves a special mention.

Alessi
22 Brook Street
London W1K 5DF
020 7491 2428
Tube: Bond Street
Open: Mon – Wed 10:30 – 6:30
Thurs – Fri 10:30 – 7:30, Sat 10:30 – 6:30

World-renowned Italian manufacturer of contemporary household accessories, Alessi finally opened its first UK store in October 2000. Located close to the capital's expensive, label-oriented Bond Street, this small, two-storeyed shop, whose alluring window displays feature some of the company's most iconic pieces, inevitably draws the passing crowds and on my visit was bustling with a good cross-section of consumers. Both the opening of the Alessi store and its swift popularity are confirmation of the British public's growing susceptibility to contemporary design.

A family-run company, Alessi was founded in 1921 by Giovanni Alessi. Since then the company has gone from strength to strength, commissioning big design names to create innovative new products for its collection. Pioneering masters such as Ettore Sottsass, Richard Sapper, Achille Castiglioni, Alessandro Mendini, Aldo Rossi, Michael Graves, Ron Arad, Andrea Branzi, Jasper Morrison, Marc Newson, Philippe Starck, Enzo Mari and Stefano Giovannoni have all brought their innovative flair to the Alessi production line.

Such a diversity of styles and philosophies could not possibly be displayed together without creating some kind of aesthetic maelstrom, so each designer has wisely been given his or her own shelf space, thus avoiding stylistic clashes and giving each style room to breathe. Here you will find Alessi's trademark cartoon-like home accessories, such as 'Coccodandy' by Stefano Giovannoni (pictured) alongside its classic cafetières and kettles; but a visit to this store will also provide a much more eclectic picture of this inspirational design company. On leaving the store, your knowledge of Alessi will have grown, but so, too, will your overdraft!

ALMA HOME

Alma Home
12–14 Greatorex Street
London E1 5NF
020 7377 0762
www.almahome.co.uk
Tube: Aldgate East
Open: Mon – Sat 10 – 6

The well-known leather-goods manufacturer Alma was established in 1940 and has grown steadily to become one of the finest producers of leather furniture, cushions and accessories. Its warehouse, workshop, showroom and offices dominate a rather dingy alley leading off the East End's Greatorex Street, but don't be put off. Persevere and you will soon find the Alma Home showroom door, and if you find it locked, don't be afraid to ask someone from the offices opposite to let you in, as Alma Home claims to be open all day.

The alluring, distinctive smell of leather hits you as soon as you enter the long, narrow showroom, and you may be tempted to settle among one of the heaped piles of cushions or on a huge suede pouffe. Venture further, though, and your amazement grows at the sheer diversity of colours and forms achievable using this most sensuous of materials – modular seating, footstools, cubes, tables, chairs, benches, storage, beanbags, sofas, shelves, rugs, floor and wall tiles, blinds and tableware are all on display. What you see is certainly not only what you get, however, because every product can be made to order in the adjacent workshops.

The Alma Home range does not consist only of in-house designs. In addition, there are pieces by such well-known designers as Ou Baholyodhin (see pp. 84 – 85), Fiona Davidson (see pp. 210 – 11) and Gitta Gschwendtner (see pp. 220 – 21). Alma Home is an international company that has developed a well-deserved reputation in its specialist field and, with a recently gained concession at Selfridges, its success looks set to continue.

ARAM DESIGN

Aram Design Ltd
3 Kean Street
London WC2B 4AT
020 7240 3933
Tube: Covent Garden
Open: Mon – Fri 9:30 – 5:30

Located on a small street between Covent Garden and Aldwych, Aram Design's vast, impressive collection is spread over three spacious floors and caters for both the domestic and contract markets.

The company has been selling contemporary furniture and lighting mainly to architects and interior designers since the 1960s. Its range largely comprises pieces from the big manufacturers – Artek, Eileen Gray Designs, Flos, Artemide, B&B Italia, Vitra, Herman Miller, Thonet and Knoll International among them – and features re-editions of classic pieces by names such as Jacobsen, Gray, Panton, Eames, Breuer, Le Corbusier, Bertoia, Castiglioni and Mies van der Rohe, as well as more contemporary names such as Arad, Morrison, Sponge, Foster and Jiricna. The list just goes on ... and on.

The public are always welcome, so don't be put off by the hushed and rather sombre, business-oriented feel of the place. Aram's busy staff will happily let you wander through this wonderful emporium of international design.

RUTH ARAM SHOP

Ruth Aram Shop
65 Heath Street
London NW3 6UG
020 7431 4008
Tube: Hampstead
Open: Mon–Sat 10–6
Sun 12–6

Setting up shop in North London's Hampstead is a risky business. Overheads in this well-heeled suburb are high and the turnover of new shops is consequently rapid. Having traded since 1995, Ruth Aram Shop (RAS) is clearly a survivor, though. Its success lies not only in its prime location on the district's main commercial street but in the broad appeal of its large product range. Most of the stock is made up of accessories, all of which are suitable for gifts. Elegant, subtle throws from Design House Stockholm, affordable contemporary glassware from LSA International and Leonardo, and slick ceramics from Fireworks (see pp. 218–19), Amano and ASA are good examples of the kind of items on display here. Furniture and lighting are also on offer, with pieces from Eileen Gray, Flos, Luceplan, Kartell, Magis, E15 and Vitra's 'Standards' range (pictured).

The shop sees a lot of passing trade as well as plenty of regulars, who are attracted by its well-chosen and affordable selection. The shop interior seems to be increasingly overstocked, though, making it feel somewhat disorganized and crowded.

AREA SQUARED
DESIGN

DESIGNERS INCLUDE:
Ou Baholyodhin
Lyndill Ferni
Louise Gates
Stuart Knock
Matthew Machouki

Area Squared Design
357 Upper Street
London N1 0PD
020 7278 9689
Tube: Angel
Open: Tues–Sat 12–6
Sun 2–6

Interior designers Stuart Knock and Lyndill Ferni set up their design business in 1999. Realizing that it would be difficult to make a name for themselves if they were always hidden away in an office, the duo took the initiative and moved into retail as a way of attracting new commissions – a bold move in the world of interior design where success is often dependent on word of mouth. In 2000, having luckily found an empty retail unit on a particularly busy stretch of Islington's Upper Street, they transformed this tiny space into

a stylish, fresh-looking shop that cuts a dash among its rather fusty antique-selling neighbours.

Stuart and Lyndill both teach interior design part time at Chelsea College of Art and Design and consequently get to see the work of a lot of exciting young designers. They appreciate the importance of supporting fresh new talent and, alongside their own range of sofas, chairs, tables and consoles, showcase the work of a handful of new graduates, hand-picked from various degree shows including the 'New Designers' at the nearby Business Design Centre. The work on display changes regularly, but on my visit, it was Louise Gates' beautiful pewterware, Matthew Machouki's white concrete plant pots and Ou Baholyodhin's perfectly proportioned wooden containers that caught my attention.

This small, pleasantly designed shop houses some truly innovative furniture and accessories, and even if you leave the place empty-handed, you are bound to feel reassured that contemporary UK design is alive and kicking.

ARIA

Aria
295 Upper Street
London N1 2TU
020 7704 1999
www.aria-shop.co.uk
design@aria-shop.co.uk
Tube: Angel or Highbury & Islington
Open: Mon – Fri 10 – 7
Sat 10 – 6:30, Sun 12 – 5

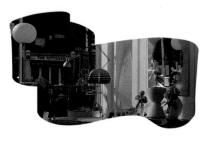

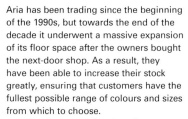

Aria has been trading since the beginning of the 1990s, but towards the end of the decade it underwent a massive expansion of its floor space after the owners bought the next-door shop. As a result, they have been able to increase their stock greatly, ensuring that customers have the fullest possible range of colours and sizes from which to choose.

The sheer quantity of products crammed into Aria is astonishing, but the overwhelming bias here is towards plastic. Aria can also probably boast one of the largest and most comprehensive collections of Alessi products in the UK, displaying them almost like religious artefacts in a series of glowing glass cabinets. Chairs figure largely, too, though once again plastic is the dominant material, with the squiggly, multifunctional

'Phantom' chair by Verner Panton (pictured) being perhaps the most striking example on offer.

The shop interior – painted wooden floor and spare white walls – is good but is lost under the welter of furniture, lighting, kitchenware and accessories. Still, everyone should be able to find something they like in Aria, even if I can't help feeling that it is quantity rather than quality that has the upper hand in this well-known Islington store.

Across the road, at No. 133, is a smaller branch of Aria (tel 020 7226 1021) selling smaller accessories such as stationery, watches and tableware.

ART, FURNITURE & INTERIORS

DESIGNERS INCLUDE:
Driade
Flos
Fritz Hansen
Knoll International
Herman Miller

Art, Furniture & Interiors
5 Ivor House
Bridge Street
Cardiff CF1 2TH
0292 040 0800
Open: Mon – Fri 9:30 – 5:30
Sat 10 – 4

Had I not known about this shop, show-room and gallery, I would never have found it. From the outside, its appearance is unprepossessing; step inside, though, and you'll find yourself pleasantly surprised by the handsome array of modern furniture on display. The owners, Tamara and Andy George, are clearly passionate about design and work hard to generate local public interest in contemporary and classic design. Displays change regularly, and there are bi-monthly exhibitions showcasing young Welsh artists.

The shop's continuous evolution helps maintain an inspiring creative buzz that seems to draw in the sometimes cautious local populace. Once inside they will find not only a large selection

from big name manufacturers such as Driade, Fritz Hansen, Knoll, Herman Miller and Flos but pieces by less well-known names, too. According to Tamara and Andy George, an investment in the 'next generation' is vital because British manufacturers are often so wary of taking risks with innovative or untested designs.

The massive Millennium developments in Cardiff Bay are stimulating lots of interest in this hitherto neglected region of the UK, and this may well encourage others to set up good, forward-thinking design shops like this one.

ATOMIC

Main Showroom
Plumptre Square
Nottingham NG1 1JF
0115 941 5577
www.atomic-online.com
enquiries@atomic-online.com
Open: Mon – Sat 9:30 – 5

Atomic 1
34b Heathcote Street
Nottingham NG1 3AA
0115 941 5330
Open Mon – Sat 10:30 – 5:30

Atomic 2
King John's Arcade
Nottingham NG1 3GR
0115 979 9940
Open: Mon – Sat 10:30 – 5:30

Several years ago Atomic's owner Simon Siegel noticed that Nottingham was in need of a shop selling contemporary product and furniture design. Would it succeed in the city? No, it would excel.

The first shop opened on Heathcote Street, selling an array of gifts and accessories, tableware, jewellery and lighting as well as a small selection of furniture. Another shop followed, slightly smaller but with much the same product range – featuring both classic and well-established manufacturers and designers. Atomic earned its success by selling highly desirable design at affordable prices.

Siegel's desire to expand Atomic's furniture range led, in January 2000, to the opening of a new showroom (pictured). The space has a good supply of natural light and opens up into a double-height room that makes it feel deceptively large, with products by Le Corbusier, Eames (pictured), Morrison, Young, Panton, Arad, Sponge, Starck and Breuer all sitting happily in the surroundings.

Atomic's three outlets all benefit from helpful and friendly staff, making a visit to the shops pure pleasure.

BABYLON

DESIGNERS INCLUDE:
Michael Anastassiades
Matthew Hilton
Rebecca Hoyes
Birgit & Christoph Israel
Simon Maidment
Torsten Neeland
Claudia Silvestrin
Vogt Weizenegger
Peter Wylly

Babylon
301 Fulham Road
London SW10 9QH
020 7376 7255
info@babylondesign.demon.co.uk
Tube: South Kensington
Open: Mon – Sat 10 – 6

Peter Wylly and Birgit Israel, owners of
the London-based lighting and accessory
company Babylon Design, opened the
doors to their first shop in October 1999.
The duo had previously made their names
designing various pieces for the likes
of the Body Shop, Habitat and The Conran
Shop, but wanted to launch a retail
space to coincide with the creation of their
own exciting new range of products.

Wylly and Israel's collection comprises
lighting and accessories from designers
such as Michael Anastassiades, Matthew
Hilton, Rebecca Hoyes, Birgit & Christoph
Israel, Simon Maidment, Torsten Neeland,
Claudia Silvestrin, Vogt Weizenegger
and Peter Wylly. Everything is displayed
in an informal loft-style space, in which
customers are free to explore and touch.
Aside from Babylon's own range,
there are a number of other pieces that
emphasize the rather New York look of
the place, such as the occasional old
leather armchair, Danish wooden cabinets
from the 1950s and 1960s, antique gilded
mirrors and glass and tableware.

With its timeless style and friendly,
attentive staff, this truly original shop is
bound to delight.

BOOM!

**BOOM!
53 Chalk Farm Road
London NW1 8AN
020 7284 4622 (mobile: 0973 114396)
Tube: Chalk Farm
Open: 12 – 6 daily
Except Wed closed**

Its easy to guess how this shop got its name. On entering, you are struck by an explosive 'boom' of light, emanating from the Castiglioni 'Arco' floorlamp that stretches elegantly across the small yet refined selling space.

The shop sells a good diversity of mainly European furniture, lighting, textiles and glassware, all dating from the 1950s to 1970s. There are the obvious design greats, of course, including Panton, Jacobsen and the Finnish glassware manufacturers iittala, but also a number of highly original generic pieces, ranging in style from the cool and conservative Scandinavian to the weird and wacky French and Italian. What makes this shop so special, though, is that everything is original, with not a reproduction in sight.

The heat from the lighting combined with the small size of the shop gives the space a rather cosy feel, and a talk with the owner, Phil Cowan, quickly convinced me of his deep passion for what he sells. A visit to BOOM! is likely to inspire and capture even the most jaded imagination.

BOWLES AND LINARES

Bowles and Linares
32 Hereford Road
London W2 5AJ
020 7229 9886
www.bowlesandlinares.co.uk
Tube: Notting Hill Gate or Bayswater
Open: Mon–Sat 11–5

Designers of furniture, lighting and accessories, Sharon Bowles and Edgar Linares opened their small Notting Hill showroom in 1997, after receiving much acclaim for their debut collection at 100% Design the previous year.

The design duo put an emphasis on the making process of their pieces, believing that 'diligence of detailing is unachievable unless done by hand.' Working in a wide range of materials such as concrete, wood, metal and glass, Bowles and Linares are committed to quality, and this is immediately apparent when you step into their shop. Greeted initially by larger pieces such as the concrete 'Cast Vessels, Vases and Bowls' and the better-known 'Espiga' floorlamps (pictured), you then come upon their slightly more affordable 'Obhetos' range of hand-blown glassware, lighting and other objects for the home.

Having said that, nothing here comes cheap, but the consistently high quality of the work and its sheer attention to detail is awe-inspiring. An investment in Bowles and Linare's work is just that, as each piece is destined to stand the test of time.

BOWWOW

Bowwow
70 Princedale Road
London W11 4NL
020 7792 8532
Tube: Holland Park
Open: Tues – Sat 10 – 6

Opened in 1997 by Ahmed Sidki, Bowwow is a unique treasure trove, discreetly tucked away on a largely residential street in Holland Park. Visiting the shop is not dissimilar to visiting the house of a friend with unimpeachable taste. The difference here, of course, lies in the fact that you can buy just about anything you see. Meticulously crafted furniture, ceramics, rugs, sculpture and objets d'art adorn the room, with handmade work from such highly talented designer-makers and artists as Vivienne Foley, Abigail Simpson, Gordon Mitchell, James Toleman, Samson Sovoye, Richard Allen and Keith Monroe.

Many of the pieces on display are designed by Sidki himself, who creates restrained, impeccably styled furniture that combines simple forms with natural colours and tactile materials.

On entering the shop, you are likely to be greeted by Sidki himself. He believes in personal service and will quite happily engage you in conversation. Be careful, though. His enthusiasm is catching, and you may end up leaving the shop with more than you – or your wallet – bargained for.

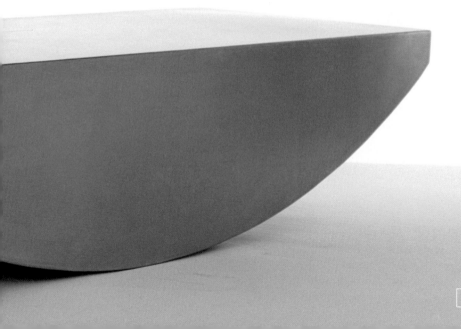

BROWNS LIVING

DESIGNERS INCLUDE:
Bowles and Linares
Stephanie Hering
Sonja Duo Meyer
Bodo Sperlein
Christian Tortu

Browns Living
26 South Molton Street
London W1Y 1DA
020 7514 0022
www.brownsfashion.com
Tube: Bond Street
Open: Mon – Fri 10 – 6:30
Thurs 10 – 7, Sat 10 – 6:30

Well-known fashion emporium Browns, which today dominates popular South Molton Street, has been a growing success ever since its launch 30 years ago. Its founder, Joan Burstein, has consistently been able to spot rising fashion talents and has showcased their work to a dedicated stream of Browns customers. Over time Browns has evolved a lifestyle philosophy focused on 'the indulgence in and enjoyment of rich, comfortable and sumptuous living', so the launch of Browns Living in 1998 must have seemed the logical next step.

Occupying a small area at the back of the main shop, the new venture displays an eclectic range of accessories for the home, that are sourced from all over the world. The selection of vases, glassware, ceramics, candles, bathroom accessories and soft furnishings changes often, but on my visit I was greeted by Bodo Sperlein's tactile ceramics (see pp. 240 – 41),

Stephanie Hering's tall, elegant ceramic vases, Bowles & Linares' beautiful glassware (see pp. 36 – 37), Sonja Duo Meyer's one-off ceramic holders and Christian Tortu's slim, slick vases (pictured), as well as by brilliantly vibrant Indian cushions and throws, quality leather picture frames, and plenty of nicely fragranced bathroom goodies.

The friendly staff are more than happy to offer advice or give information about the products on display. Although Browns continues to be dominated by fashion, it is refreshing to see clothing and products so well combined as well as to discover some fresh design names.

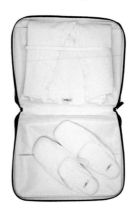

CARDEN CUNIETTI

DESIGNERS INCLUDE:
Joe Colombo
Ghost House
Murano

Carden Cunietti
83 Westbourne Park Road
London W2 5QH
020 7229 8630
www.carden-cunietti.com
cc@carden-cunietti.com
Tube: Westbourne Park or Royal Oak
Open: Mon – Sat 10 – 6

Audrey Carden and Elenora Cunietti are the names behind this quirky Notting Hill shop. The interior-design duo, who undertake a variety of international design projects from their offices across the road, wanted to open a small shop selling a variety of items that they felt would embody their unique design ethos. The result is a shop that brings together an eclectic array of objects sourced from around the world, with one-off period pieces rubbing shoulders with objects of more modern design.

Craftsmanship and individuality are the outstanding characteristics of every piece. Resisting the temptation to create a uniform house style, the owners have built up a collection that is as diverse and contradictory as their own likes and passions and which is nevertheless surprisingly down-to-earth. Selling mainly glassware, ceramics and accessories, the shop also features occasional items of furniture and lighting. Bamboo cutlery, jewelled frames, Japanese crackleware, vibrant Murano vases, Joe Colombo stacking glasses and Ghost House quilts are just a taste of what you might expect to find.

If you are searching for that special touch of luxury or individuality, then Carden Cunietti is the perfect place to start.

CAZ SYSTEMS

DESIGNERS INCLUDE:
Ron Arad
Artemide
Flos
Kartell
Luceplan
Magis
Marc Newson
Herman Miller
Jasper Morrison
Rexite
Philippe Starck
Zanotta

Caz Systems
18/19 Church Street
Brighton BN1 1RB
01273 326 471
Open: Mon – Sat 10 – 6

Caz Systems is Brighton's major showcase for big-name design. About half the shop is devoted to furniture, with Flos, Artemide, Kartell, Luceplan, Magis, Rexite, Zanotta and Herman Miller just some of the names on offer to Brighton's well-heeled forty-somethings and big-spending trade professionals. The other half of the shop is given over to more affordable home accessories, with glassware, clocks, and plenty of kitchenware from the likes of Arad, Morrison, Starck and Newson. Owner Neil Davies also runs a lighting design and installation service, with an impressive clientele that includes the Imperial War Museum, so it's not surprising to find that lighting plays a large part in the shop, too.

Shopping here can be a bit predictable, but an almost-complete extension into the shop next door may well enable Davies to offer a slightly more adventurous range. All the same, if it's big names you're after, Caz is the place to find them.

CENTRAL

Central
33 – 35 Little Clarendon Street
Oxford OX1 2HU
01865 311 141
www.central-furniture.co.uk
Open: Mon – Sat 9:30 – 6
Sun 11:30 – 5:30

Before Central opened in 1997, Oxford's design-conscious inhabitants had to travel to London if they wanted to buy well-designed, good-quality furniture and accessories. Since then, though, they have been able to visit this large, centrally located shop, where owner Geoff Taylor sells a good selection of the usual suspects in international design.

Central is a great stop both for homewares and gifts, with price tags to suit every budget. In particular, fans of the affordable LSA International glassware range (pictured) will have a field day here.

Furniture and lighting on display includes pieces by Starck, Arad, Hilton, Eames, Le Corbusier, Jacobsen, Noguchi, Mies van der Rohe, Panton, Bertoia and Castiglioni, some of which are given pride of place in the glass-fronted window display.

This is very much a mainstream shop and the selection is inevitably a little predictable. In a small city like Oxford, however, a good, general design shop such as this one is to be welcomed and cherished.

CENTURY

Century
68 Marylebone High Street
London W1 3AQ
020 7487 5100
Tube: Baker Street
Open: Tues – Sat 10 – 6

Century Design opened its tiny basement shop on Marylebone High Street in 1996, selling mainly American furniture, lighting and accessories from the 1950s to the present. Fans of classic American designers such as Eames, Nelson, Noguchi and Risom will be pleased to learn that Century sells both new re-editions as well as some highly desirable originals.

The shop has a good cross-section of products, presented not as a series of isolated, unconnected pieces, but as part of a wider contextual setting, creating a comfortable fusion out of the diversity of styles on offer. This strategy helps the customer develop an overall picture in his or her mind of the look and feel a particular object may create in the home.

Apart from the classics, very little contemporary North American design is showcased in the UK, so it's both refreshing and encouraging to see work from the likes of a young Canadian firm called Pure Design, who commission fresh ideas from such talented designers as Proctor Rihl, Stephen Burkes and Douglas Coupland. Accompanying their shelving units, tables and accessories are an assortment of rugs and runners by Karim Rashid and a range of handmade soft furnishings from New York's Jonathan Adler.

The overall feel of the shop is intimate, and owing to the small size, it's easy to spark up a conversation with the friendly and knowledgeable staff or with owner Andrew Weaving. Should you be after a particular piece, Weaving's insight into American design, especially mid-century modern, may well prove invaluable.

CHAPLINS OF LONDON

DESIGNERS INCLUDE:
B&B Italia
Rolf Benz
Cassina
Desalto
Flexform
Fritz Hansen
Kartell
Ligne Roset
De Sede

Chaplins of London
477–507 Uxbridge Road
Hatch End, Pinner
Middlesex HA5 4JS
020 8421 1779
www.chaplins.co.uk
Train: Hatch End
Open: Tues – Sat 10 – 6

Chaplins of London is a family-run retailer that boasts the largest selection of contemporary designer furniture in the UK, including representative pieces by many of the biggest European manufacturing names. Situated on the city's outskirts, the company's showroom allows customers to interact with products in a way that is generally impossible in smaller outlets. Chaplins fully appreciates that in view of the high cost of its offerings, potential customers will often want to gain an all-round visual and tactile experience of a piece before committing to a purchase.

The large manufacturing names that Chaplins represents, such as Cassina, Fritz Hansen, B&B Italia, Kartell, Desalto, Flexform, Rolf Benz, Ligne Roset (see pp. 112 – 3) and De Sede may not mean much to the average customer, but the often famous designers behind these companies – including Philippe Starck, Piero Lissoni, Antonio Citterio, Vico Magistretti, Le Corbusier, Gerrit Rietveld, Frank Lloyd Wright, Arne Jacobsen, Ludwig Mies van der Rohe, Charles and Ray Eames, Marcel Breuer, and Ron Arad – may inspire a more creative appreciation of exactly what's on offer here.

The spacious, glass-fronted showroom creates a calm environment for the customer to explore and contemplate. The efficient staff are more than happy to help and advise, but know just when to give a customer time and space when the crunch comes.

Chaplins' considerable product choice, coupled with their excellent and reliable customer service, has attracted an international clientele. With another smaller store recently opened in Central London, the company looks set to keep on growing.

NIGEL COATES

By now everyone should have heard of Nigel Coates, the controversial, avant-garde architect who designed the Body Zone sculpture for the ill-fated Millennium Dome. Beyond his architectural projects at Branson Coates Associates and his running of the architecture course at the RCA, Coates now also has a small shop above his practice's office – a low-key, gallery-like space that showcases his vibrant, eclectic collection of furniture, glassware and accessories. There are silky, colourful vases and bowls designed for Simon Moore, rugs for Kappa Lambda, chairs for Lloyd Loom, sofas for Hitch Mylius, jewellery collections for Tateossian, and Coates' own sportswear line. The Clerkenwell shop brings Coates' 21st-century interior styling together in one place, rather like an exhibition. Considering it's the work of one of the most innovative designers of new millennial Britain, any purchase will probably be a worthwhile investment.

Nigel Coates
1 Honduras Street
London EC1Y 0TH
020 7336 1400
www.bransoncoates.com
info@bransoncoates.com
Tube: Barbican or Old Street
Open: Mon – Fri 10 – 5:30

THE CONRAN SHOP

The Conran Shop
Michelin House
81 Fulham Road
London SW3 6RD
020 7589 7401
www.conran.com
Tube: South Kensington
Open: Mon, Tues, Fri 10 – 6
Wed – Thurs 10 – 7
Sat 10 – 6:30, Sun 12 – 6

55 Marylebone High Street
London W1M 3AE
020 7723 2223
Tube: Baker Street
Open: Mon – Sat 10 – 6
Thurs 10 – 7, Sun 12 – 6

The Conran Collection
12 Conduit Street
London W1R 9TG
020 7399 0710
Tube: Oxford Circus
Open: Mon – Sat 10 – 6:30
Thurs 10 – 7:30, Sun 12 – 6

Since Terence Conran opened the first Conran Shop on London's Fulham Road in 1973, the store has consistently maintained its commitment to provide stylish, modern homewares to a well-heeled and design-conscious clientele. Its success stems from a thorough understanding of what its customers want. Eschewing the 'avant-garde' for the 'modern', The Conran Shop concentrates on a core of beautifully made, understated designs, covering every aspect of the home interior, with thousands of products sourced from all over the world. At the heart of the shop, however, is the Conran Collection itself – sophisticated design at its serene best. This elegance is matched by the shop's calm – and calming – environment, in which everything is beautifully displayed. The staff are friendly and are always on hand should you need help or advice, but they won't pester you if you don't.

Terence Conran has branded a way of life – comfort, style and enjoyment without pretension. If ever you feel bereft of any of these elements, then a trip to The Conran Shop is recommended.

THE CUBE

The Cube
14 Holland Street
London W8 4LT
020 7938 2244
www.thecube.co.uk
info@thecube.co.uk
Tube: High Street Kensington
Open: Mon–Fri 9–6
Sat 11–6

Anyone attracted by the harmony of pure clean lines and natural luxurious fabrics will find the understated products on offer at The Cube refreshingly satisfying. As the name of the shop suggests, The Cube's collection is inspired by the 'fresh, fine and simple' qualities of the cubic form. The 'Luxury Meets Purity' range of sofas and chairs successfully combines refined and unobtrusive elegance with comfort and texture, while managing to avoid any starkness implied by its obvious cubist influences. Similarly, the 'Invisible' range of tables, chairs and consoles is made entirely from Plexiglass, but while these pieces possess a distinct sculptural appeal, they remain decidedly functional. In addition to furniture, The Cube also offers some lighting and a selection of beautiful, natural linen and pashmina curtains, bedcovers, cushions and throws, together with various other interior accessories. The majority of The Cube's pieces are designed in-house, appealing to those aiming to achieve a complete 'look'.

The Cube's premises are located at the end of a quiet stretch of shops off busy Kensington Church Street. The space, however, is surprisingly small and is somewhat irritatingly divided in two by a partition wall, separating the tiny display area from the design desks and office area to the rear. Compensating for this lack of showspace, however, are a good catalogue, freephone mail-order service and excellent website, allowing customers to view and buy the complete collection.

DESIGNERS GUILD

Designers Guild
267 – 271 & 275 – 277 King's Road
London SW3 5EN
020 7351 5775
www.designersguild.com
Tube: Sloane Square or South Kensington
Open: *Showroom*
Mon – Tues 9:30 – 5:30
Wed – Thurs 9:30 – 6
Fri – Sat 10 – 6
Open: *Shop*
Mon – Tues 9:30 – 5:30
Wed – Sat 10 – 6, Sun 12 – 5

Designers Guild has been supplying quality interior products for some thirty years. Seemingly oblivious to passing fads and fashions, owner-founder Tricia Guild has consistently applied her distinct creative vision to the selection, mixing old with new to create a retail environment that is quite different from the rather predictable offerings so often found elsewhere.

The company's own well-known range of furnishing fabrics, wall coverings, upholstery and bed linen wholesales throughout the world, and there's certainly an impressive collection on offer in the King's Road showroom, with designs ranging from subtle checked linens to vibrant, luxurious silks, all made, of course, to the highest standard. To accompany the range, the Designers Guild shop – just a few doors away from the showroom – has a generous selection of carefully chosen interior products, including glassware, ceramics, tableware, smaller accessories and some furniture. The beautiful range of products, many exclusive to Designers Guild, are contemporary without being overtly avant-garde.

The shop itself is an appealing space. Well-displayed, sensuous products, an abundance of natural light and helpful, knowledgeable staff make it hard to walk out empty-handed.

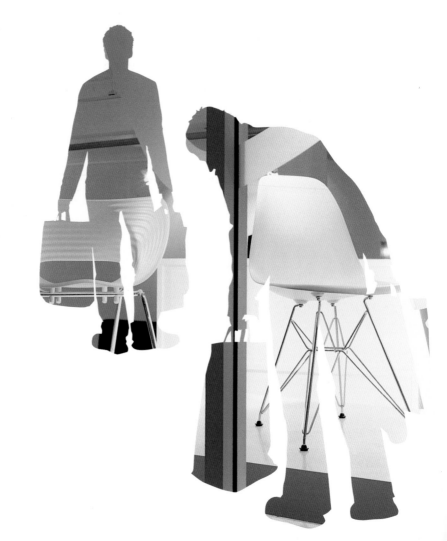

DOMANE INTERIORS

Domane Interiors
Union House
5 Bridge Street
Leeds LS2 7RF
0113 2450 701
www.domaneinteriors.com
Open: Mon – Fri 9 – 5:30
Sat 10 – 5

In recent years inner-city Leeds has undergone something of an urban renaissance, and the smart new housing developments have helped foster local interest in, and demand for, modern design. In 1998 two recent Leeds graduates in 3-D design, Ben Ritson and Ashley Thornton, spotted the burgeoning market for high-quality, well-designed furniture and accessories and seized the opportunity to set up in business together under the name of Domane Interiors.

In January 2000 Domane moved to larger premises, enabling Ritson and Thornton to expand their product portfolio, which today includes the likes of B&B Italia, Artifort, Vitra, Driade,

MDF Italia, Hitch Mylius, Kartell, Flos and Artemide. The shop successfully blends the classics with newer designs, effortlessly marrying, for example, Eames with Arad (pictured) and Paulin with Platt & Young. Also selling lighting and some ceramics and glassware, Domane has managed to create a coherent 'look' that nevertheless preserves the products' integrity within the space. A visit to this shop is warmly recommended.

DOMUS

Domus
Constance House
117 High Street
Norton, Stockton-on-Tees
TS20 1AA
01642 649 411
Open: Mon–Sat 10–5

Since opening in October 1998, Domus has established itself as the one and only place in the North East to buy contemporary furniture, beds, lighting, glassware, ceramics and bathroom and kitchen accessories. Situated a little way out of Stockton in the rather genteel suburb of Norton, the shop provides a pleasant, fresh environment – white and sky-blue walls, wooden floors and plenty of natural light – in which even the most design-wary of local residents

can discover some of the best things contemporary design has to offer.

Owner Emma Kench successfully blends affordable accessories such as kitchenware by Alessi, Koziol and Authentics, glassware by LSA International, tableware by Ella Doran (see pp. 214–15) and ceramics by Michael Sodeau with more expensive pieces such as ceramic lights by Julie Nelson (see pp. 234–35) and Babylon Design, George Nelson's 'Marshmallow' sofa for Aliva and glass tables by Fiam. Especially encouraging was the presence of the beautifully crafted wood furniture of Germany-based designers E15 (pictured).

Staff are friendly, knowledgeable and helpful, making a visit to the shop illuminating as well as unintimidating. It's to be hoped that Domus' success will inspire other creative entrepreneurs in the otherwise design-barren North East.

GEOFFREY DRAYTON

Geoffrey Drayton
85 Hampstead Road
London NW1 2PL
020 7387 5840
www.geoffrey-drayton.co.uk
Tube: Warren Street or Euston Square
Open: Mon–Sat 10–6

Though situated on an ugly road dominated by mainly run-of-the-mill furniture retailers, this 'modern furniture' retail emporium lures you inside by its intriguing window display. The shop is a well-known name in the design world, bringing big-name pieces to both the public and trade. Furniture, storage, lighting, beds, bathroom fittings, accessories and glassware from such large European manufacturers as B&B Italia, Cassina (pictured), Fontana Arte, Flos, Flexform, Kartell and Lumina adorn not only the showroom space but also the many product files that customers are able to scour. Like many large retailers, the shop may be geared towards trade professionals with big wallets, but the public is welcome, too, and many affordable designs are available for more modest budgets.

Geoffrey Drayton can offer anything from small accessories to an entire interior package, making this a perfect place to buy for those with little time to shop around. An out-of-town branch is located at 104 High Street, Epping, Essex CM16 4AF (tel 01992 573 929).

EAT MY HANDBAG
BITCH

Eat My Handbag Bitch
6 Dray Walk
The Old Truman Brewery
91–95 Brick Lane
London E1 6QL
020 7375 3100
www.eatmyhandbagbitch.co.uk
info@eatmyhandbagbitch.co.uk
Tube: Aldgate East or Liverpool Street
Open: Daily 11 – 7

The provocative name Eat My Handbag Bitch always raises eyebrows, and the shop has consequently attracted a lot of attention since its launch in May 1999. At that time, the shop had a rather cluttered feel, but since then down-to-earth owners George and Georgina have worked hard to get the shop just right and have achieved deserved recognition for their supply of original 1950s, 60s, 70s and 80s furniture and lighting.

As with every shop dealing in originals, it is difficult to specify exactly which pieces will be available during any one visit. When I went there, the curving, organic form of Charles and Ray Eames' 1948 'La Chaise' had the limelight spot in the front window. Behind it, a nine-metre-long segmented sofa by Swiss company De Sede snaked across the interior, with a brown leather 'Swan' chair by Arne Jacobsen poised elegantly beside it. Having climbed the short staircase to the mezzanine, I found curvaceous designs by Jan Ekselius, Olivier Mourgue, Pierre Paulin and Verner Panton, with Florence Knoll, Achille Castiglioni, Gae Aulenti and Joe Colombo also making an appearance. Various lights were dotted around, as well as rugs and artwork. Accessories generally play a smaller role here, but at the time of my visit original Hornsea ceramics and some retro clocks were on offer.

While they are keen to sell to a broad clientele, the owners find that a lot of their rarer pieces go over to America, with the British public remaining typically reserved when it comes to purchasing anything risqué. It's well worth breaking this backward attitude by making a trip to this welcoming East London shop – you might surprise yourself.

ECLECTIC

Eclectic
202 Brick Lane
London E1 6SA
020 7613 3009
www.eclecticfurniture.co.uk
mack.duff@virgin.net
Tube: Aldgate East
Open: Daily 10 – 6

Eclectic opened at the end of 1999 in a small shop on the East End's Brick Lane. An array of what owner Clifford Mackduff describes as 'loft-style' furniture originals is crammed into the two floors of the shop. There seems to be some bias towards leather, with plenty of sofas and armchairs packed in back-to-back. Many pieces are generic, with some classics from the likes of Eames and Le Corbusier coming into stock, too. The majority of pieces are sold through the trade, but Clifford hopes that sales to the public will increase as the shop becomes better known.

As in many shops, there is a constant battle with space. Eclectic, though, has been filled to capacity without resorting to stacking, and the white walls, mirrored back wall and simple use of uplighters have worked to make the space feel bigger. The selection is continuously evolving, so on any one visit remember that you may not find exactly what you want. If your mind is set on one particular piece, it may be worth calling Eclectic in advance or checking out the website.

ENGLAND AT HOME

England at Home
22b Ship Street
Brighton BN1 1AD
01273 205 544
www.englandathome.co.uk
Open: Mon–Sat 10–6
Sun 12–5

Owned by Therese and Bob England, this Brighton shop has a manager sporting the surname England, too, so it hardly comes as a surprise to discover that the products on display here are all from... well ...England. On sale are mainly accessories, including plenty of tableware, glassware, lighting, artwork, as well as a few pieces of furniture, providing a good overall selection for the contemporary 'English home'.

The central location means the shop benefits from a lot of passing trade, with the lovely curved-glass shop front allowing for a highly alluring window display. The handsome wooden flooring also provides an attractive setting in which to display such desirables as lights by Dixon and Babylon Design, ASA ceramics, LSA International glassware and 'Gabriel' lamps by Brighton-based designers Gecko. If you are unable to visit the shop, all of the products can be viewed and purchased through the website, with a full wedding list service available as well. Another shop selling smaller accessories that are suitable for gifts is located a few doors down at 32 Ship Street (tel: 01273 738 270).

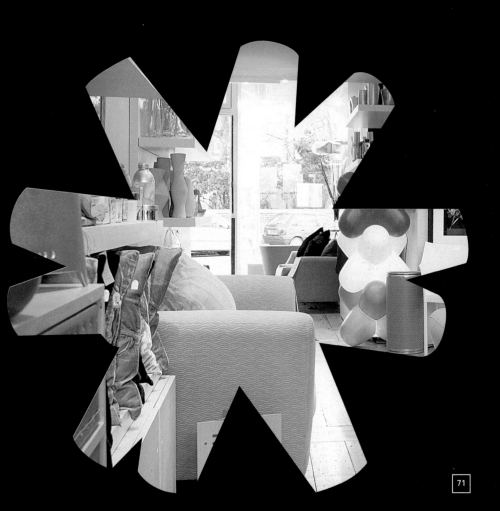

DESIGNERS INCLUDE:
ASA
Babylon Design
Tom Dixon
Gecko
LSA International

De La Espada
60 Sloane Avenue
London SW3 3DD
020 7581 4474
www.delaespada.com
Tube: South Kensington
Open: Mon–Sat 10–6
Wed 10–7, Sun 12–5

Perfection is something that all the staff at De La Espada consistently aim to achieve. This understated furniture store simply oozes luxury, comfort and quality, with beds, sofas, chairs, tables, cabinets, storage and accessories all designed in-house and manufactured in Spain. Wood is the core material here, and attention to quality of colour and grain is responsible for the sensuous look and feel of the products. Everything is handmade to the highest specification, with nothing released from the factory until it meets the expected standard. Every piece is available in oak, cherry or walnut, with the highest-quality leather, Ultra suede or fabric used for the upholstery.

This spacious and elegant Sloane Avenue shop was opened in 1996, but since then it has doubled in size to meet demand. Its serene interior is composed of unobtrusive variations of chocolate, cream, white and grey, with gentle background music adding to the soothing mood. De La Espada's clean, smart and modern aesthetic comes at a price, of course, but bear in mind that lasting quality design is never cheap.

FALCONER

DESIGNERS INCLUDE:
Le Corbusier
Dualit
Ferrious
Eileen Gray
Guzzini
Inflate
Mathmos
Ludwig Mies van der
Rohe

Falconer
362 Muswell Hill Broadway
London N10 1DJ
020 8365 3000
Tube: Highgate, then 134 bus
Open: Mon – Tues 9 – 6
Wed – Sat 9 – 7, Sun 10 – 6

Setting up a contemporary lifestyle shop like Falconer in a London suburb is a risky business since there's no knowing whether it will catch on with local customers. However, this glass-fronted shop has clearly hit the right buttons.

Located on a busy roundabout in Muswell Hill, the shop attracts a constant flow of passing trade, owing both to its prime retail positioning and the large, diverse selection of products on sale. Falconer has succeeded in targeting the everyday shopper by making good design accessible. The selection combines best-sellers like Dualit toasters and Mathmos lava lamps with some quirkier accessories from Inflate, Guzzini and Ferrious (such as Claire Norcross's 'Eight Fifty' lamp, pictured) as well as a few classic pieces of furniture from Le Corbusier, Eileen Gray and Mies van der Rohe. A large range of affordable homewares, bags, jewellery and cards are also in stock, making this a good place to come for a stylish, affordable gift. There is also a smaller Falconer in Crouch End at 11 Topsville Road, London N8 (tel 020 8348 4848).

FANDANGO

Fandango
17 Essex Road
London N1 2SE
020 7689 8778
www.fandango.uk.com
Tube: Angel
Open: Wed – Sat 11 – 6
Sun 12 – 5
Mon and Tues by appointment
(tel 07979 650805)

Owners Henrietta Palmer and Jonathan Ellis opened Fandango in April 1999 in a small retail space just a stone's throw from Islington Green. The duo source original furniture, lighting and accessories from the 1950s, 60s and 70s, restoring them where necessary and exhibiting them together, regardless of period, style or origin. There is, however, a definite emphasis on European design, with Danish rosewood furniture, vibrant Holmegaard glassware and Italian pendant lighting leading the field on my visit.

The space is illuminated mainly by natural light, and the white-painted brick walls give the shop the feel of a small New York loft apartment. The quantity of stock is always changing due to fluctuations in the supply of, and demand for, original pieces. On my visit, the shop felt surprisingly uncluttered for an outlet of this sort, with everything given sufficient space and equal pride of place.

There is a general assumption that all original pieces command high prices. Although this is true for the established classics, you may well find yourself a bargain here, with many accessories and retro goodies selling with affordable price tags.

Every Saturday, the owners try to restock the space with newly sourced items, ready for the design-hungry shoppers who pass through their doors. Visiting on this day, then, is likely to give you the widest possible choice. You can also put the owners' sourcing skills to the test, as they are willing to help search for any particular piece or style you may have a hankering for. They may not be able to perform miracles, but given the number of regulars that frequent the shop, they must be doing something right.

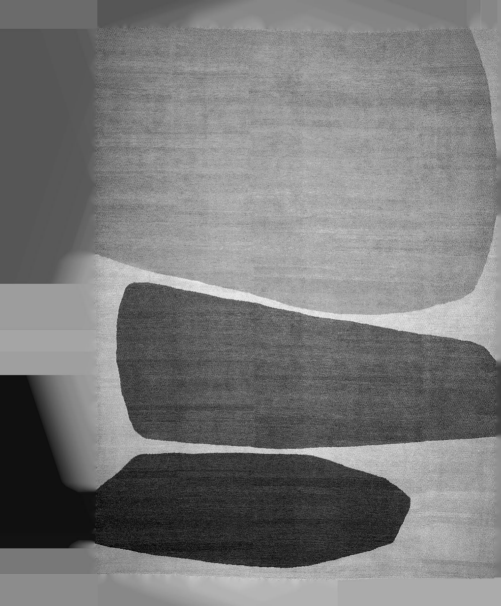

DESIGNERS INCLUDE:
Kate Blee
Georgina von Etzdorf
Christopher Farr
Romeo Gigli
Gary Hume
Rifat Ozbek
Michael Sodeau
Michael Young

Christopher Farr
212 Westbourne Grove
London W11 2RH
020 7792 5761
www.cfarr.co.uk
info@cfarr.co.uk
Tube: Notting Hill Gate
Open: Mon – Sat 11 – 6

During the late 1980s, Christopher Farr quickly established himself as one of London's most sought-after designers of quality contemporary rugs. Originally trained as an artist, Farr has a painter's eye for colour and form, which he puts to good use in his designs. A selection of his work – produced in annual collections – can be seen in his small Notting Hill shop, where the rugs cover the walls almost like paintings.

Farr's creations can measure anything up to about four by three metres, so, given the restricted space of the shop, it's clearly impossible for him to display all of the collection in one go. However, Farr has cleverly provided postcard images of every available design, with the added benefit that potential buyers can mull over their choice at home.

Making the right decision is crucial, since the rugs don't come cheap. However, the cost seems fully justified once you realize that every rug or flat weave is made from hand-spun, hand-dyed highest-quality Anatolian wool, lending each piece its own individual fluctuations of colour, texture and form.

In addition to Farr's own creations, the shop also displays rugs commissioned from leading artists and designers such as Kate Blee, Georgina von Etzdorf, Rifat Ozbek, Romeo Gigli, Gary Hume, Michael Young and Michael Sodeau. The same high quality is assured, and any of these rugs will provide a striking – and lasting – accompaniment to a contemporary domestic interior.

FERRIOUS@HOME

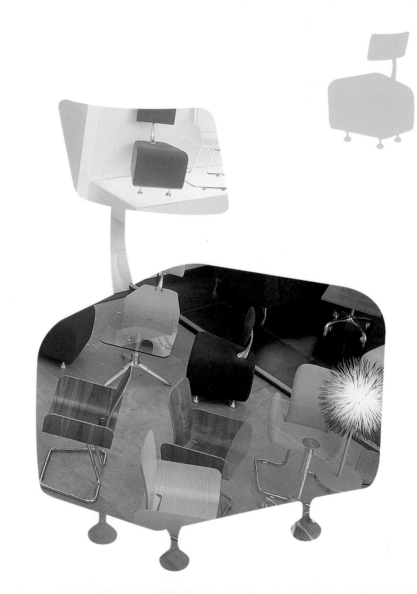

Ferrious@home
Arch 61, Whitworth Street West
Manchester M1 5WQ
0161 228 6880
www.ferrious.co.uk
enquiries@ferrious.co.uk
Open: Tues – Sat 11 – 6

Partners Jeremy West and Paul Tempest formed the Manchester-based design group Ferrious in 1993. Initially working on commissioned furniture and lighting, the duo went on to create production pieces for the trade. Having won attention at numerous international contemporary design shows, the company's innovative products also caught the imagination of the increasingly design-conscious public back at home. It was a logical progression, therefore, to adapt the company's slick showroom space for the retail market.

Occupying a stunning double-height railway arch on Whitworth Street West, Ferrious has put its entire collection on display, including the famous 'Lush' chair, originally designed for Manchester's fashionable Lush Restaurant, and the 'Ru' chair, made for The Rock, London's exclusive Embankment bar. Newer additions are the 'Tuck' and 'Bel' series, with which the company launched its move into domestic furniture. Claire Norcross's 'Eight Fifty' lamp and Tom Kirk's 'Spike' and 'GS Chandelier' (see pp. 228 – 29) provide some brilliant illumination.

Greeted by an enthusiastic but down-to-earth team of staff, you are assured a warm welcome here, making a visit to the shop nothing less than an inspirational pleasure.

FLOW

Flow
1–5 Needham Road
London W11 2RP
020 7243 0782
galeries.flow@ukgateway.net
Tube: Notting Hill Gate
Open: Mon–Sat 11–6

In May 2000 the enthusiastic and welcoming Yvonna Demczynska and Vivien Fotiadis opened Flow in a light and airy space that had previously housed a contemporary art gallery. The duo brought together a mixed collection of contemporary applied arts that, they believe, reflects a movement away from the stark minimalism of the 1990s towards 'softer designs inspired by nature's organic curvilinear forms'.

Flow represents an impressive array of designer-makers specializing in ceramics, jewellery, metalwork, wood, textiles and glass, and exhibits their work on simple, round platform-shelving spaced around the gallery walls. The interior acts as a calm, understated backdrop to the work, with the abundance of natural light giving full value to the beautifully crafted detailing of each piece. Soft, fluid glass bowls by Marianne Buus, minimal and modernist-inspired ceramic vases by Bridget Tennent, delicate wooden vessels by Liam Flynn and wittily engineered metalwork by Hans Stofer (pictured) are just a few examples of the many unique and varying creations this Notting Hill gallery can offer.

Flow occasionally holds shows of a particular designer's work, and these are always worth checking out. It is hugely encouragingly to find a space dedicated to exhibiting and promoting the works of so many lesser-known talents, and it's to be hoped that Flow will blaze a trail for other similar galleries to follow.

FUNCTION

Function
1st Floor
12 Greatorex Street
London E1 5NF
020 7426 0666
www.ou-b.com
function@ou-b.com
Tube: Aldgate East
Open: Mon–Fri 10–5:30

Ou Baholyodhin, the owner of Function and the designer behind the majority of its offerings, converted his one show-room into a retail outlet in October 1999 in response to growing public interest in his work. Ou has designed interiors for the retail, restaurant and hotel industry all over the world, including the UK's trendy K-bars, as well as product designs and installations for big-name

names such as Kenzo, Joseph and Donna Karan. Function's location may seem unprepossessing – a converted industrial block in a dingy alley a few minutes' walk away from Brick Lane – but the slick, ultra-cool, Zen-like space within never fails to impress. Ou's entire collection is on display: refined, understated furniture, lighting and tableware that exploits materials such as stainless steel, glass, teakwood, suede and horsehair to both sensual and functional effect. His consistent use of simple forms and clean lines can be found in all of his products, from linear stainless-steel vases to voluptuous nesting tables.

Though often dubbed 'minimalist,' Ou creates a style that is neither cold nor sterile. With work this good, a visit to Function is seriously recommended.

GRAHAM & GREEN

Graham & Green
4, 7 & 10 Elgin Crescent
London W11 2JA
020 7727 4594
www.grahamandgreen.co.uk
Tube: Notting Hill Gate
Open: Mon–Sat 10–6
Sun 11–5

164 Regents Park Road
London NW1 8XN
020 7586 2960
Tube: Chalk Farm
Open: Mon–Sat 10–6
Sun 11:30–5:30

340 Kings Road
London SW3 5UK
020 7352 1919
Tube: Sloane Square
Open: Mon–Sat 10:30–6:30
Sun 12–6

Ever since opening in 1974 on Notting Hill's Elgin Crescent, Antonia Graham's 'modern ethnic' store Graham & Green has seen an increasing number of customers through its doors as knowledge of its whereabouts has spread.

Antonia has always used a simple yet effective philosophy when selecting her stock and that is to sell home accessories, furniture and clothing that are inspirational and individual and, most importantly, that are things that she loves.

Her shops are stuffed with an incredibly diverse array of objects, ranging from lacquer bowls and Morrocan tea glasses to goatskin rugs and mohair throws. Indeed, it's rather like visiting the house of a well-travelled friend as you browse through the numerous fascinating and desirable items sourced from around the world. The difference is that you have the option to buy!

With no importance placed on designer names, one is guided solely by one's instincts and purchasing decisions become as personal as Antonia's. For those of you fed up with the monotony of high street shopping and global producers, try Graham & Green as an eclectic retail bolthole.

DESIGNERS INCLUDE:
Erwan and Ronan Bouroullec
Anna Castelli Ferrieri
Achille Castiglioni
Lucienne Day
Robin Day
Alan Fletcher
Gioia Meller-Marcovicz
Ross Menuez
Lisa Norrinder
Verner Panton
Pierre Paulin
Simon Pengelly
Ettore Sottsass
Sori Yanagi

Habitat
196 Tottenham Court Road
London W1P 9LD
020 7631 3880
www.habitat.net
Tube: Tottenham Court Road
Open: Mon – Wed 10 – 6, Thurs 10 – 8,
Fri 10 – 6:30, Sat 9:30 – 6:30, Sun 12 – 6

Other stores nationwide
Call 0845 60 10 740
or go to www.habitat.net

Designer and entrepreneur Terence Conran opened the first Habitat on London's fashionable Fulham Road in 1964. Conran's visionary aim was to revolutionize the way ordinary people perceived modern design, presenting innovative yet affordable products in a refreshing, unstuffy retail environment. The formula – unquestioned today – was a risky one in the early 1960s, but since then Habitat has become one of the UK's great retail success stories, with more than 40 shops in this country alone, as well as stores worldwide.

Habitat has always had to face the challenge of sustaining its youthful image in order to maintain its appeal to its prime clientele – the design-conscious urban young. Most recently, Habitat's head of design, Tom Dixon, has once again redefined and upgraded the store's image,

while remaining loyal to the company's original retail philosophy. To accompany the excellent Habitat-designed core collection of furniture, lighting, glass, china, kitchenware, tableware, bathroom accessories and bed linen, Dixon has reissued a number of iconic designs that are now '20th-century classics' – including pieces by Robin Day (pictured), Ettore Sottsass, Verner Panton, Pierre Paulin, Achille Castiglioni, Anna Castelli Ferrieri (pictured), Lucienne Day, Sori Yanagi and Alan Fletcher (pictured). While paying homage to the designs of the past, however, the store has certainly not lost sight of today's movers and shakers, commissioning designers of the calibre of Erwan and Ronan Bouroullec, Ross Menuez, Simon Pengelly, Lisa Norrinder and Gioia Meller-Marcovicz to produce exciting new product lines.

The recent appointment of Matthew Hilton as head of furniture will no doubt further enhance the creative energy and direction of the company. In a world obsessed with corporate buyouts and fashion-following, it is encouraging to see a large store like Habitat not only maintaining but also developing its distinctive identity.

CONTEMPORARY GALLERY, HARRODS

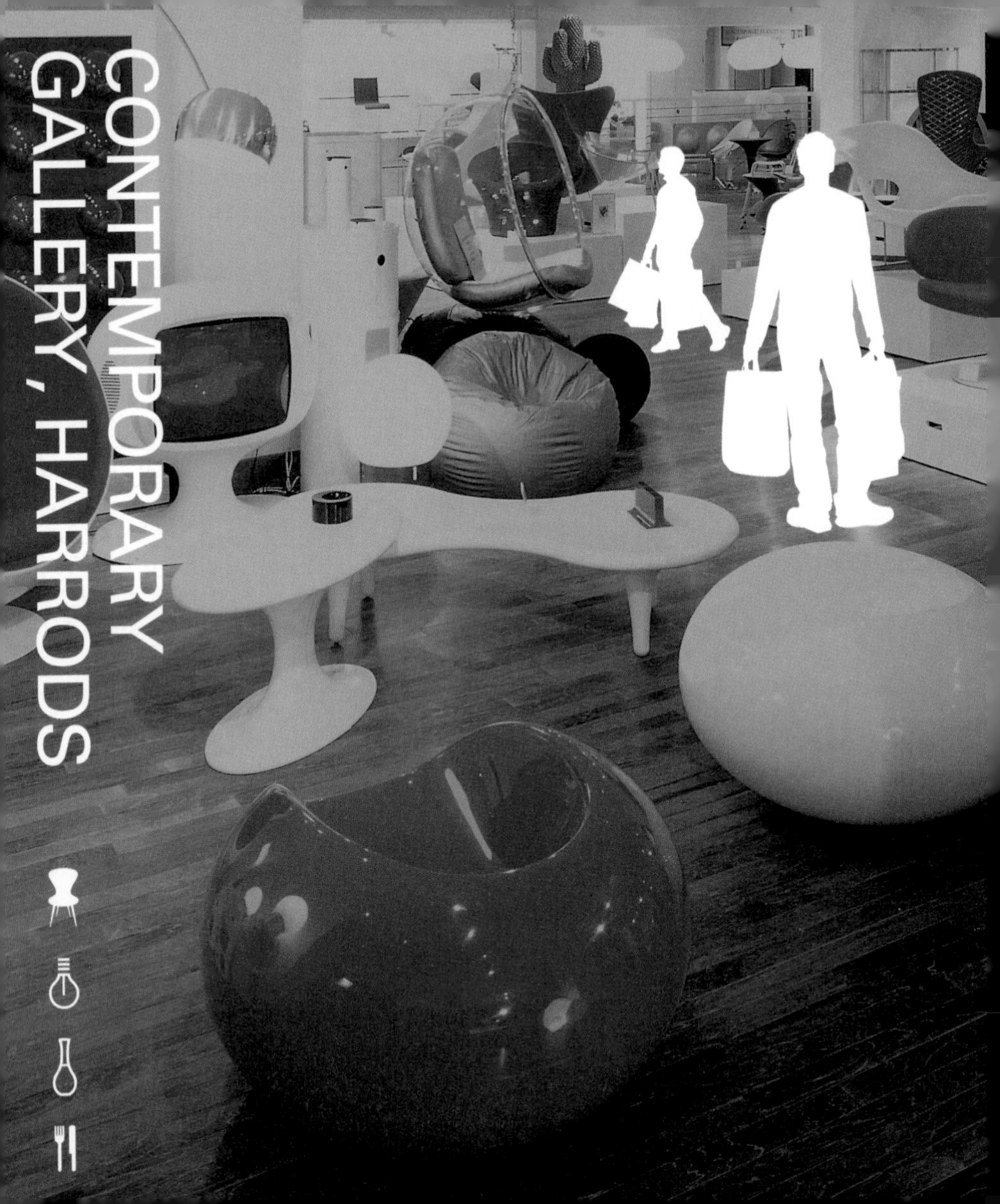

Since 1928 luxury retailer Harrods has dedicated its entire third floor to furniture, specializing in high-quality, traditional styles, with very little space given over to contemporary designs. Recently, however, homewares director Anne Pitcher and furniture buyer Norbert Killmaier have responded to the growing public interest in contemporary furniture, producing a fresh, new concept for the department that nevertheless remains responsive to their client base.

In May 2000 their concepts became reality with the unveiling of the inspirational 'Contemporary Gallery', which offers an outstanding selection of furniture, lighting and accessories, not only from the pioneering 'cult' designers of the past but also from today's fresh, cutting-edge talents. Pitcher and Killmaier are both originally from fashion backgrounds, and the collection has undergone a degree of styling: classic icons are effortlessly combined with newer pieces, creating an overall context that successfully sidesteps the 'do-not-touch' sterility that mars many other furniture stores.

To mention all of the offerings in this huge department would be impossible, especially when they are all so good. With a similar fresh approach in evidence in the second-floor accessories department, Harrods has positioned itself squarely behind forward-thinking modern design. Never known to do things by halves, Harrods' successful metamorphosis may well pave a path for other stores to follow.

DESIGNERS INCLUDE:
Ella Doran
Hackman
Heals
Ligne Roset
LSA International

Heals
196 Tottenham Court Road
London W1T 7LQ
020 7636 1666
www.heals.co.uk
Tube: Goodge Street
Open: Mon–Wed 10–6
Thurs 10–8, Fri 10–6.30
Sat 9:30–6:30, Sun 12–6

Call for details of other stores

Heals, well-known retailer of quality furniture and interior products, has been selling stylish, contemporary wares to a steady stream of customers for almost 200 years and has built itself into a staple of the shopping circuit. All four stores – on London's Tottenham Court Road and Kings Road, and in Kingston and Guildford – have prime retail locations and all benefit from plenty of passing trade. The Heals style might be best summed up as elegant contemporary. The high-quality furniture, rugs, beds, furnishing fabrics, bed linens and vast range of home accessories are neither garishly cutting-edge nor sombrely conservative but are instead somewhere comfortably in between, successfully appealing to a diversity of consumers. Many items are exclusive to Heal's, but all share high-quality workmanship and attention to detail. The choice of products is extensive in all departments, and there are prices to suit most budgets.

NOEL HENNESSY FURNITURE

Noel Hennessy Furniture
6 Cavendish Square
London W1G 0PD
020 7323 33609
www.noelhennessy.com
shop@noelhennessy.com
Tube: Oxford Circus
Open: Mon – Fri 10 – 6
Sat 10 – 4

Noel Hennessy opened this furniture shop in Cavendish Square early in 1998. Although the shop looks rather small from the outside, inside is a spacious salesroom spread over two floors, displaying furniture, lighting, accessories and artworks, with a huge portfolio of designs from which to choose. If big manufacturing names such as B&B Italia, Alivar, Hitch Mylius, Zanotta, Fiam, Porro and Artemide mean little or nothing to you, then the words 'minimalist', 'slick', 'refined', 'quality' and 'Italian' may give a better idea of what is on offer here,

though the pieces are displayed without the bland impersonality that such adjectives might usually imply. Noel Hennessy Furniture runs its own interior-design service, and its designers have managed to give the pieces a distinctly warm and laid-back feel by selecting earthy colours and natural woods and bathing the pieces in ambient light.

The friendly staff allow customers to browse freely but are more than happy to help if advice is needed. The company sales pitch here might well be 'great design made unintimidating', and the salesroom is certainly an excellent place for those for whom interior design seems mysterious or pretentious.

The Home
Salts Mill
Victoria Road
Saltaire
Bradford BD18 3LB
01274 530 770
Open: Daily 10–6

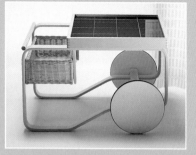

Salts Mill has quickly established itself as one of Bradford's premier attractions. Housed in a mid-19th-century converted factory, this unique venue comprises not only the world's largest collection of work by Bradford-born artist David Hockney but also a gallery shop, traditional furniture shop, restaurant and an excellent design store – The Home.

Owing to the immense size of their premises, The Home's owners, Robin and Pat Silver, have been able to set up an extraordinarily comprehensive collection. The sheer range of furniture, lighting, glassware, ceramics, table and kitchenware, and accessories on offer makes The Home feel almost like a museum of design, with everything displayed on plinths or in cases with 'Do Not Touch' signs adjoining them. The difference, of course, is that you are encouraged to buy, with plenty of help on hand from the smiling, attentive staff.

As for the products, if seating from Mies van der Rohe, Jacobsen, Aalto, Breuer, Bertoia, Eames, Panton, Colombo, Sottsass, Rietveld, Castiglioni, Arad and Starck doesn't get your design juices going, then I don't know what will! Glassware from Ritzenhoff, iittala, LSA International, Roericht and Nils Landberg, and tableware from Caterina Fadda (see pp. 216–17), Enzo Mari, Bonapart, Rosenthal and Brian Keaney are just a taster of the incredible range of accessories available.

With such copious coverage of modern and contemporary design on offer, and the added bonus of all the other attractions at Salts Mill, a visit to The Home is warmly recommended.

IKEA

Ikea
Ikea Brent Park
2 Drury Way
North Circular Road
London NW10 0TH
020 8208 5600
Tube: Neasden,
then a 20-minute walk
Open: Mon–Fri 10–10
Sat 9–7, Sun 11–5

Ikea Croydon
Old Power Station
Valley Park
Purley Way
CR0 4U2
020 8208 5601
Tramlink or bus 289 or 455
from central Croydon
Open: as above

Other stores nationwide
Call 020 8208 5607 for branches
Opening hours vary

Founded by Ingmar Kamprad in Sweden in 1943, the blue-and-yellow-branded global giant Ikea has become the largest furniture chain in the world, employing nearly 40,000 people and turning over billions of dollars every year. From the outset, the company has specialized in making simple, well-designed modern furniture affordable to ordinary people with ordinary incomes. To fulfil this objective, the company has constantly questioned the usual givens of manufacturing and has successfully come up with alternatives that reduce costs to a minimum. Massive production runs, flat-packing to reduce transportation and storage expenses, and home-assembly are all factors that contribute significantly to lower unit costs, which Ikea dutifully passes on to its consumers. This achievement, together with some simple, modern, functional designs, more than explains the company's success.

With a staggering range of items on offer, covering every aspect of interior furnishing, it's hard not to feel overwhelmed by the stark, no-frills approach to consumerism evident in Ikea's suburban, warehouse-style superstores. However, Ikea's simple interior solutions are often to be commended, and have clearly won the loyalty of a growing band of people with 'more taste than money'. With plans for significant UK growth, Ikea clearly has faith that their success will continue to blossom.

Indish
13 & 16 Broadway Parade
Crouch End N8 9DE
020 8340 1144
Tube: Archway then 41 or W5 Bus
Open: Mon – Sat 10:30 – 5:30

Since opening at No.13 Broadway Parade in 1996, Indish has been selling beautiful, colourful, natural-looking linens alongside a carefully selected range of contemporary lighting and accessories. Lacking the space needed to introduce cutting-edge furniture to its repertoire, a new shop was acquired at No.16, which opened in November 1999.

With its white walls and wooden floors, No.16 has established an identity quite separate from that of its parent shop. Crammed into a small space are recent pieces by such big names as Dixon, Newson, Arad and Starck, together with work by less well-known designers such as Catarina Fadda (see pp. 216 – 17), Fireworks (see pp. 218 – 19), Sponge (see pp. 242 – 43), El Ultimo Grito (see pp. 244 – 45) and Spaced Out. Encouraging as this diversity is, the rather jumbled presentation makes one wonder whether Indish's buyer simply loves everything or is just hugely indecisive. With this choice and quality, however, who really cares?

DESIGNERS INCLUDE:

Ron Arad

Tom Dixon

Caterina Fadda

Fireworks

Marc Newson

Spaced Out

Sponge

Philippe Starck

El Ultimo Grito

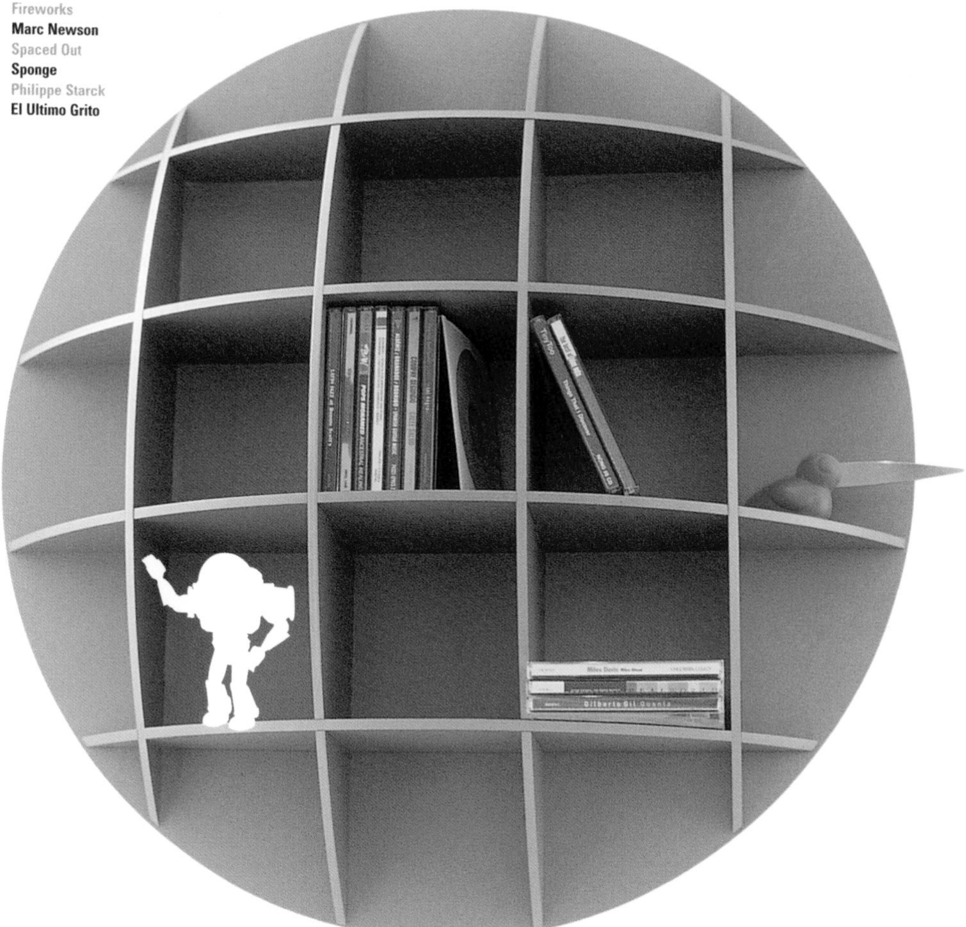

INHOUSE

Inhouse Edinburgh
28 Howe Street
Edinburgh EH3 6TG
0131 225 2888
www.inhousenet.co.uk
Open: Mon – Fri 9:30 – 6
Thurs 10 – 7, Sat 9:30 – 5:30

Inhouse Glasgow
24–26 Wilson Street
Glasgow G1 1SS
0141 552 5902
www.inhousenet.co.uk
Open: Mon – Fri 10–6
Thurs 10 – 7, Sat 9:30 – 5:30

Inhouse first opened in Edinburgh in 1982 and since that time has grown to become one of Scotland's leading design stores, with a branch opening in Glasgow in 1988. Both shops sell the same broad product range, but owing to lack of space are able to display only a small percentage. All the same, visitors to the shop are likely to be able to view a varied mix of pieces from designers such as Lovegrove, Starck, Morrison, Thun and Rossi, among many others.

Inhouse tries to satisfy all ages, tastes and budgets, but the main part of the business is the high-end furniture pieces that attract design professionals, first-time buyers and the contract market. However, both shops also have an accessories section that occupies about a third of the available space, selling a large selection of books, glass, china and kitchenware from the likes of Alessi, such as the classic 'La Conica' cafetière by Aldo Rossi (pictured), iittala, Arzberg, Hackman and David Mellor. Although Inhouse's shop spaces are somewhat cluttered, there is an impressive choice of items, making them good places to look for gifts.

The staff are friendly and happy to offer advice. Their aim is to take the hassle out of fitting out your home so that you can enjoy the experience, not dread it! Other services include a full interior contract provision as well as wedding-list and mail-order services.

ISOKON PLUS

DESIGNERS INCLUDE:
Barber Osgerby
Associates
Marcel Breuer
Hans Sandgren Jakobsen
Michael Sodeau
Sori Yanagi

Isokon Plus
Turnham Green Terrace Mews
London W4 1QU
020 8994 0636
www.isokonplus.com
Tube: Turnham Green
Open: Mon – Sat 11 – 5:30

In 1935 British entrepreneur Jack Pritchard founded the Isokon Furniture Company, at the time a daring, forward-thinking initiative. Pritchard's vision gained added credibility with the appointment of Bauhaus architect Walter Gropius as the firm's 'Controller of Design'. It was Gropius, too, who suggested the hiring of Marcel Breuer, former 'Master of the Carpentry Workshop' at the Bauhaus, as the company designer – a move that catapulted the firm into the forefront of international modernism.

The furniture created by the Isokon team focused on the use of plywood, a material with which Pritchard had had previous experience. Breuer's extraordinary designs gave rise to a classic collection that remains at the heart of the company's repertoire today.

In 1982 Pritchard asked specialist makers Windmill Furniture to take over both production and sales of the Isokon pieces, and since then the new owners have consistently added to the core collection, developing and commissioning new products from contemporary designers, such as Barber Osgerby Associates.

In 1999 Windmill set up its own retail outlet, Isokon Plus, above its Chiswick workshops. This calm, quiet showspace houses all of Breuer's Isokon classics and the newer pieces by Michael Sodeau and Barber Osgerby Associates, together with other innovative plywood works from the likes of Sori Yanagi and Hans Sandgren Jakobsen.

With such illustrious beginnings, it would have been easy for Isokon to have grown complacent. The ongoing introduction of new, cutting-edge pieces, however, looks set to create a new generation of design classics.

KUME

Kume
20 Bond Street
Brighton BN1 1RD
01273 602 667
www.brightonpages.co.uk/kume
Open: Mon – Sat 10 – 5
Sun 12 – 5

Designer Sally Ure Reid opened this tiny
shop on Brighton's bustling Bond Street
in December 1999. The shop acts as a
selling space for some wonderful
handmade products from an assortment
of designers and craftspeople, many of
them local, including ceramics from Wendy
Jung, Geraldine McGloin (see pp. 232–33)
and Marc Boase (see pp.204–205), as
well as tableware from Parisians tse & tse.
Sally herself produces many of the
products on offer, including aluminium
vases, chunky wooden coffee tables and
handmade paper vases and lights.

The owner is influenced by the Japanese notion of wabi – the 'perfection of the imperfect'. Everything for sale is unique, a statement that would normally imply expense, but which here means quite the opposite. Sally is alert to the fact that high prices would alienate her shop from the majority of the Brighton public and also believes that by selling handcrafted, 'organic-contemporary' and affordable pieces by recently graduated or young designers, she will attract customers interested in owning the one-offs normally associated with costly commissioning. Providing individuality is clearly Sally's objective here, in a 'retail space offering a fluid selection of design and art'.

THE LIFESTYLE COMPANY

The Lifestyle Company
17 Lamb Street
London E1 6EA
020 7247 3503
Tube: Liverpool Street
Open: Tues – Fri 12 – 6
Sat 11 – 6, Sun 10:30 – 6

The historic Spitalfields Market continues to hold its ground on the Commercial Street divide between City and East End. No longer the thriving market it used to be – except perhaps at weekends – this huge covered space still houses shops and restaurants in the units that line the building. Of these, one of the most interesting is the Lifestyle Company, a treasure trove packed with unusual furniture and lighting originals dating from the 1960s, 70s and 80s.

The shop's offerings are continually changing, with newly sourced or restored pieces quickly taking the place of any outgoings. The origin of the items is diverse, though the majority appear to come from European countries. The array of chandeliers and pendant lights form an impressive overhead collection that can be admired, for example, whilst testing the comfort factor of a characterful old leather sofa. Chromed tubular-steel seating, chunky marble coffee tables and vibrant stackable chairs are other examples of the various looks on offer here.

The shop normally attracts more people at weekends, so browsing can be difficult at this time. A weekday visit is a better option if you need more attention from the staff as well as time and space for serious contemplation. But don't take too long to decide; there's a strong chance that whatever you're humming and hawing over may be gone by the next day!

LIGNE ROSET

Ligne Roset
23–25 Mortimer Street
London W1T 3JE
020 7323 1248
www.ligne-roset.com
www.lrwestend.co.uk
Tube: Goodge Street
Open: Mon–Sat 10–6
Except Thurs 10–8

Ligne Roset City
62–82 Commercial Road
London E1 1NN
020 7702 2124
ww.ligne-roset-city.co.uk
Tube: Aldgate East
Open: Mon–Sat 9:30–6
Except Thurs 9:30–8

In May 2000 one of the leading French furniture manufacturers, Ligne Roset, took the bold step of moving into a Central London location. The company already occupies a showroom in West London's Chiswick and have also just opened a new showroom on Commercial Road in East London, but the progression to a more accessible outlet in the heart of the city has proved a success, if the positive reviews that greeted the launch are anything to go by.

The spacious Central London shop is spread over two floors – a perfect size to house the company's large collection of unobtrusive, clean-cut furniture, lighting and accessories. The well-lit airy space with wooden floors and white walls provides an elegant backdrop for an array of sofas, chairs, beds and storage, designed by the likes of Pascal Mourgue, Didier Gomez, Claude Brisson and Peter Maly. More recently, Ligne Roset has begun to introduce a slightly more cutting-edge feel to its stock of lighting and accessories, commissioning pieces from young, avant-garde French designers. Vibrant rubber lights by Adrien Gardère, ethereal stainless-steel-mesh lights by Arik Lévy (pictured), wall-mounted vases by Ronan Bouroullec and sandblasted moulded-resin vases by Sophie Suchodolski have given the company's image a more experimental, contemporary look.

The friendly, laid-back staff will assist where needed, otherwise leaving you to browse in this relaxed retail outlet. If you don't live in London, check the website for your nearest dealer.

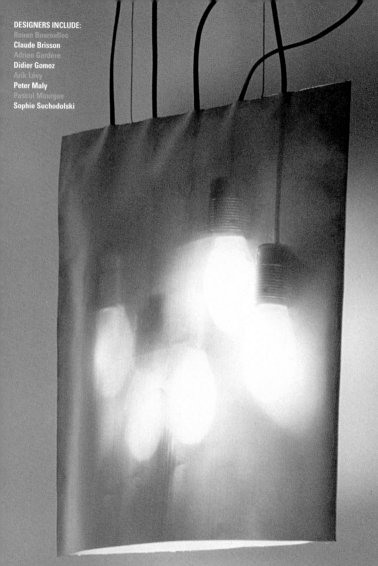

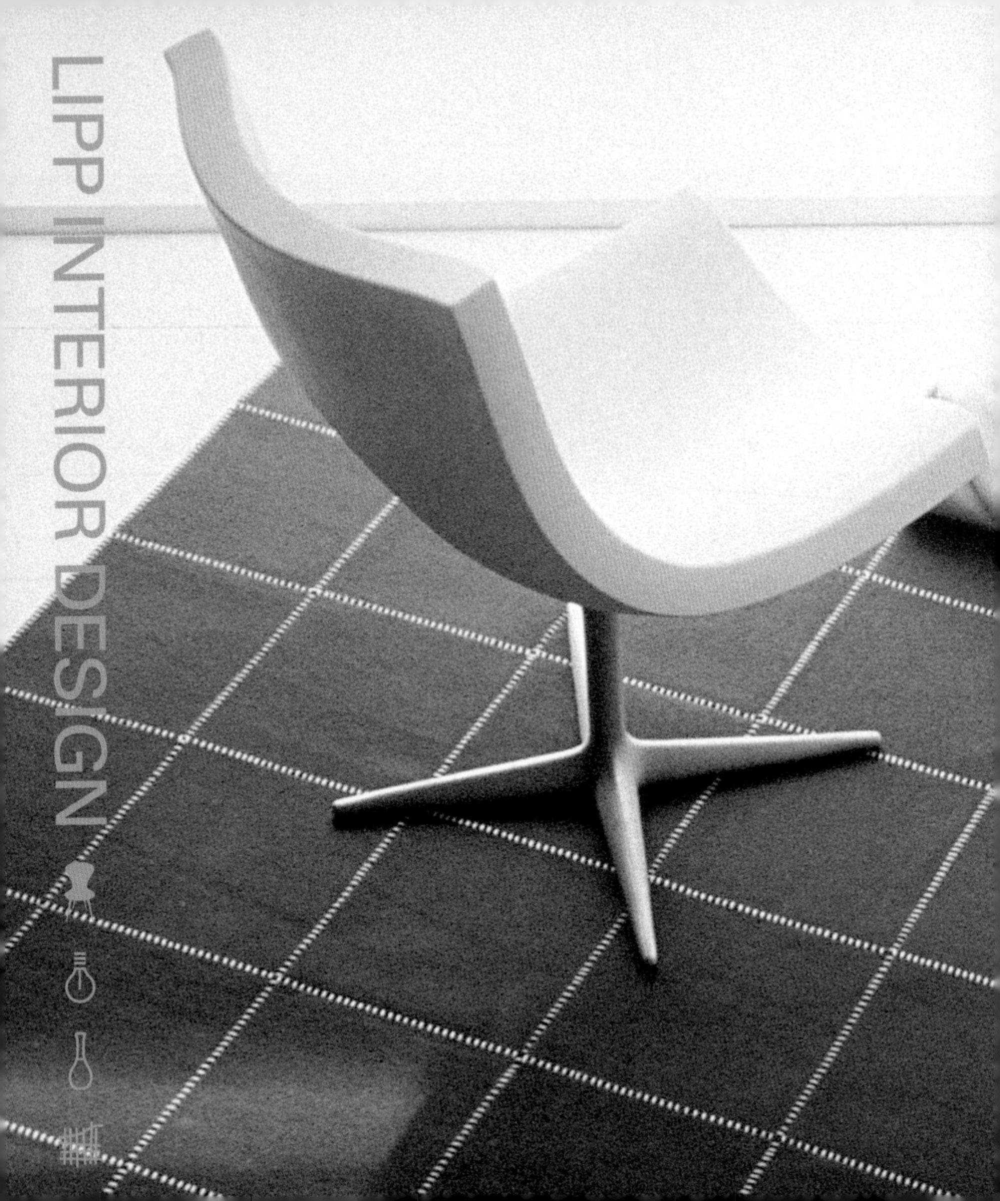
LIPP INTERIOR DESIGN

Lipp Interior Design
118a Holland Park Avenue
London W11 4UA
020 7243 2432
Tube: Holland Park
Open: Mon–Fri 10–7
Sat 11–7

Since opening in August 1997 in Holland Park, one of London's wealthiest and most sought-after districts, Lipp has been providing a full interior-design service to the domestic and contract markets. Their shop acts both as showroom for the trade clientele and as a retail outlet for those of us who are, perhaps, only after a single item. Deceptively small from the outside,

the shop's main hub is located in the basement, reached via a spiral staircase. Here you will find a selection of contemporary European furniture and lighting that combines traditional quality and refinement with the increasingly popular modern look.

The slick contemporary forms beloved by so many style magazines predominate, with big names such as B&B Italia, Maxalto, Zanotta, Living Divani (pictured), Baleri-Italia, Rexite and lapalma all represented. There is also an excellent selection of fabrics and flooring materials on display. Should you have any difficulty in finding what you are after, the friendly, helpful staff will do all they can to help.

Living
Mechind House
16–17 Lionel Street
Birmingham B3 1AQ
0121 236 1722
Open: Mon–Sat 10–6
Sun 10–5

Located in a rather plain showroom on the ground floor of an office building, Living is Birmingham's only contemporary design store. Originally an interior-design company, it opened to the public in July 1999. Although the clientele is made up predominantly of design professionals, the staff offer a friendly welcome to the public, too – something that is reflected in the broad product range that encompasses both affordable glassware and accessories and high-end furniture and kitchen fittings.

The showroom itself is not huge, but there is much more on offer than the products on display. Living can boast a huge range of items from European manufacturers such as Vibieffe, Artemide, Flexform, Jesse, Felicerossi and Living Divani as well as a good selection of the classics. Despite such variety, products remain on the safer side of contemporary living, with a bias towards tasteful woods and muted colours.

Living prides itself on 'a growing collection of furniture [whose] strength lies in its simplicity of form brought about by careful design and attention to detail'. If what you are looking for is an interior that is able 'to withstand passing trends and fashions', then a visit here is recommended.

LIVING SPACE

Living Space
36 Cross Street
London N1 2BG
020 7359 3950
www.intospace.com
Tube: Angel or Highbury & Islington
Open: Mon–Sat 10:30–6
Sun 11–5

Owner Spencer White opened this crisp, slick shop on a side street just off Islington's busy Upper Street in April 2000. Spotting the ongoing growth in the popularity of 'loft-living' in London, White wanted to sell a selection of contemporary furniture that would occupy these open-plan spaces. With so many of the capital's other furniture retailers offering the big-name manufacturers, Spencer was keen to introduce pieces that are not quite so well known.

The shop from the outside appears a lot smaller than it really is, the fresh white walls of the front room opening up into a much larger 'loft-style' space at the back. Displayed throughout is a careful selection of furniture, including sofas, tables, chairs, beds and many flexible storage units. The emphasis seems to be on modular furniture that can be customized to suit a client's particular needs. Living Space offers a home-visiting service to advise on sizes and finishes, as well as on whether or not a particular piece is appropriate for the intended space. This helps ensure that the client is always happy with the end result, as there is obviously no room for error with customized pieces.

Living Space attracts customers who are after slick, well-designed, quality furniture for their new urban dwellings. With its clean, fresh appearance and fantastically helpful and welcoming staff, this shop makes for a stress-free, even soothing shopping experience.

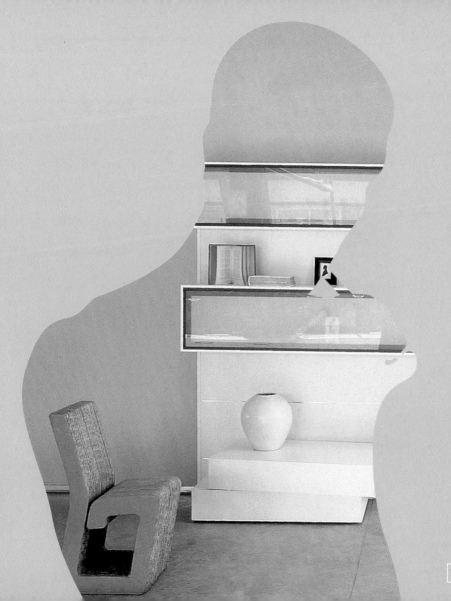

Lloyd Davies
14 John Dalton Street
Manchester M2 6JR
0161 832 3700
Open: Mon – Sat 10 – 6
except Thurs 10 – 7
Sun 12 – 5

Known as the Conran of the North, Bob Lloyd-Davies has won himself an enviable reputation in the increasingly design-conscious city of Manchester since opening his first shop there in 1997.

Lloyd Davies, the store, occupies a building that was previously owned by Habitat, with two generously sized floors that feel markedly different in style. On the ground floor is a smaller, more affordable selection including table and glassware from Ella Doran (see pp. 214 – 15), LSA International, Arzberg and

John Rocha as well as books, clocks, cards and other miscellaneous items. The basement is altogether more serious, housing furniture, lighting and linen by names such as Le Corbusier, Gray, Castiglioni, Eames, Noguchi, Dixon, Starck and Hilton. Large manufacturers are represented, too – with Cassina and B&B Italia sofas, Flos, Artemide and Luceplan lighting, and Driade and Montis chairs being just a snippet of what is on offer. What caught my eye above all, though, was the work of Paris-based Catherine Memmi, whose contemporary-rustic designs would fit well into any loft or barn conversion, traditional or contemporary.

The staff are all design graduates and are enthusiastic and knowledgeable about what they sell. That, married with the range, makes a trip to Lloyd Davies a highly pleasurable one.

LOFT

Loft
24 – 28 Dock Street
Leeds LS10 1JF
0113 305 1515
www.loftloft.com
Open: Mon – Sat 10 – 6
Except Thurs 10 – 8
Sun 12 – 5

Housed in a 19th-century warehouse conversion in Leeds' Riverside district, Loft is an impressive 3,000-square-foot design store selling both contemporary and classic furniture, lighting and home accessories. Since Mac Maclean opened Loft in the summer of 2000, it has enjoyed a steady stream of design-hungry consumers who are continually awe-struck by the vast space and the range of products on offer.

The exposed brick walls and beams, together with the unusual floor of pea gravel set in epoxy resin, provide a wonderfully textural backdrop for furniture and lighting from SCP (pp. 168 – 69), Cappellini, Vitra (pp. 192 – 93), Fritz Hansen, Knoll, Artemide, Flos, Luce Plan and Ingo Maurer. Equally guaranteed to raise one's pulse are designs from the likes of Jasper Morrison (pictured), Matthew Hilton, Andrew Stafford, Tom Dixon, Marcel Wanders, Ron Arad, Arne Jacobsen, Le Corbusier and Verner Panton. For those in search of a quick, less costly design fix, glassware, ceramics, tableware and bathroom fixtures by pioneers such as Stelton, Rosenthal, Hackman, and iittala also grace the displays.

The staff at Loft are knowledgeable and helpful, leaving one quietly confident that this formidable design store will be able handle your interior needs to a level that matches the high quality of its products.

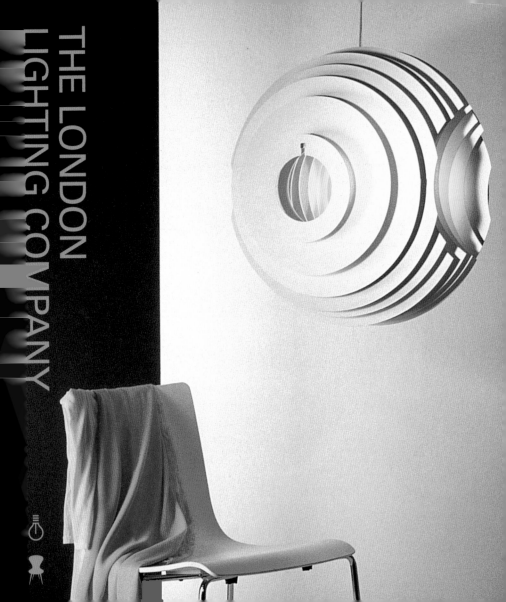

THE LONDON
LIGHTING COMPANY

DESIGNERS INCLUDE:
Achille Castiglioni
Ernesto Gismondi
Tobias Grau
Ferruccio Laviani
Michele de Lucchi
Ingo Maurer
Isamu Noguchi
Paolo Rizzatto

The London Lighting Company
135 Fulham Road
London SW3 6RT
020 7589 3612
Tube: South Kensington
Open: Mon – Sat 9:30 – 6
Sun 12 – 5

'Their name says it all' is what I would write if I were restricted to a single-line review of this well-known Chelsea store. The London Lighting Company has been trading for some 28 years, establishing itself as one of London's best outlets for big-name lighting design.

From the outside the shop looks quite small. Inside, however, the showroom opens up, revealing a dazzlingly impressive galaxy of lights of all shapes, sizes and kinds – uplighting, downlighting, ambient lighting, spot lighting, task lighting and occasional lighting. Designers represented include such illustrious names as Achille Castiglioni, Ernesto Gismondi, Tobias Grau, Ferruccio Laviani ('Supernova' pictured), Michele de Lucchi, Ingo Maurer, Isamu Noguchi and Paulo Rizzatto. More than 1,000 different designs are held in stock for dealing with both domestic and project clients worldwide. In order to break up the monotony so often felt in lighting shops, some classic furniture pieces have recently been added, giving the lighting spatial context. Should you feel the need for expert advice, there are plenty of helpful, experienced and design-trained staff available to 'help you see the light'.

Getting the lighting right is vital in any interior, so it is advisable to aim for the best, which undoubtedly means a trip to SW3.

LUNA

Luna
23 George Street
Nottingham NG1 3BH
0115 924 3267
www.luna-online.co.uk
info@luna-online.co.uk
Open: Mon – Sat 10 – 5:30

Since 1994 owner Paul Rose has been shifting a rapidly changing array of original 1950s, 60s and 70s glassware, tableware, lighting, ceramics and furniture. Some of this he sources from fairs and markets, but quite a good amount is brought directly to him by the public.

Luna is a tiny shop, but its corner location allows plenty of natural light to show off its vibrant window display. Like any shop dealing in originals, it is unpredictable in what it sells. However, Rose does sell an impressive semi-permanent collection of colourful glassware from Murano, Whitefriars (pictured), Mdina and Holmegaard as well as equally impressive examples of Hornsea, Midwinter and Portmeirion ceramics. Owing to lack of space, furniture is unable to play a big role here, but on my visit Harry Bertoia and Robin Day chairs made an appearance.

Luna is a great place to find unusual pieces at surprisingly affordable prices, and the friendly atmosphere makes it a pleasure to visit for additions to the house, gifts or simply a browse.

Louis McCullough opened MAC in March 1998, in response to the growing local demand for leather sofas and armchairs to furnish the huge number of Clerkenwell loft conversions that even now continue to appear. The desire to acquire a characterful, uniquely worn sofa is for many the only interior option; the look and feel of brand-new leather pales in comparison. Louis sources these rarer, one-off finds for a faithful band of customers, reconditioning and repairing them in his warehouse before exhibiting them in his showroom space, which is strikingly located on a busy corner of Clerkenwell Road.

Louis is not interested in sourcing 'designer' pieces, especially with demand for old-leather products being so high. He accordingly offers a straightforward sales policy: if you want a different piece, he will exchange or buy back your purchase at any time for the same price that you paid, depending on the item's condition and resale likelihood.

As turnover of pieces is high, the shop's appearance changes often, so don't be dismayed if it sometimes looks cluttered. Providing leather furniture for the Match bars and many other domestic and commercial interiors, MAC has established itself as a leader in the field of unique leather seating.

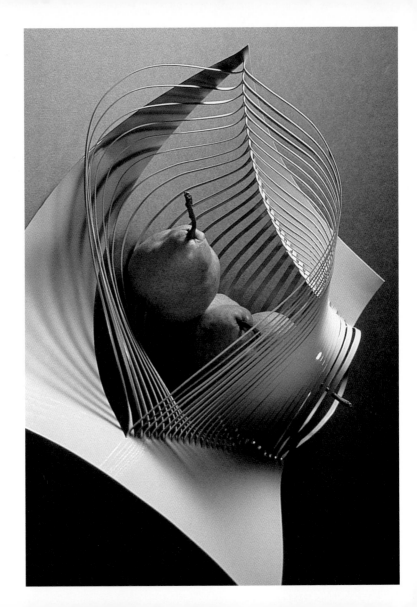

DESIGNERS INCLUDE:
Peter Allen
Antonis Cawdew
Ane Christensen
Alan Dunlop
Chris Healey
Nick Hodder
Simon Tsouderous

Makers
40/40a Snowsfield
London SE1 3SU
020 7407 7556
Tube: London Bridge
Open: Tues – Sat 9:30 – 5:30

Alan Dunlop opened Makers on a quiet inner-city street near London Bridge Station in 1999. He has created a warm, cosy exhibiting space, the focus of which is the work of locally based designer-makers.

A furniture-maker himself, Dunlop is all too aware of the difficulties facing designers specializing in one-off, hand-crafted products; lack of workshop space and expensive specialist machinery, he believes, can often impede creative experimentation and progress. Taking a leap of faith, he has given about a dozen talented makers – including Ane Christensen (pictured), Chris Healey, Nick Hodder, Peter Allen, Antonis Cawdew and Simon Tsouderous – the opportunity of

using the shop's workshop basement to create beautifully crafted offerings that are then sold in the gallery upstairs. Not working to specific commissions, the makers have complete creative freedom – a set-up that Dunlop strongly believes promotes the best and most innovatory work.

Makers is developing a reputation for high-quality furniture, lighting and accessories and attracts a mixed bunch of 'word-of-mouth' customers. Makers also acts as the designers' agent, so it's also possible to commission specific pieces. Anyone fed up with the onslaught of mass-produced and globally marketed goods should certainly make a trip to SE1.

MASON

Mason
70 North Street
Leeds LS2 7PN
0113 242 2434
www.masonfurniture.com
info@masonfurniture.com
Open: Mon – Fri 9:30 – 5:30
Sat 10 – 5

Robert Mason launched this shop in Leeds' up-and-coming Northern Quarter in October 1998. With its rather quirky selection of furniture from Alivar, Insitu, Desalto, such as the shelving (pictured), Sponge, Le Corbusier, Corin Mellor and the infamous, outrageously OTT Mark Brazier-Jones, Mason's focus here is decidedly on quality before affordability. Not everything is expensive, though, with some price tags as low as £100. When the owner first opened the shop, he was afraid that its large, showroom-like space would intimidate potential customers, and, to counteract this possibility, he tried to give the shop a relaxed, laid-back feel. The attractive contemporary art (from Angus McArthur's Snow Gallery; tel 0113 245 6464 or e-mail www.snowbrand.co.uk) on the walls, the sound of a radio playing, and the smell of coffee brewing may all help in this respect, but above all it is Robert Mason's own friendly and helpful attitude that is most likely to put people at their ease.

DAVID MELLOR DESIGN

David Mellor
4 Sloane Square
London SW1 8EE
020 7730 4259
www.davidmellordesign.com
Tube: Sloane Square
Open: Mon – Sat 9:30 – 6

David Mellor is a well-known, award-winning cutler who has been producing top-quality, elegant classics for many years. The Sheffield-based designer originally trained as a silversmith, but established his international reputation only after shifting his talents to cutlery.

Mellor's excellent range can be found in many good design outlets and kitchen shops across the UK, but the best place to go, of course, is his very own shop in London's Sloane Square. Spread over two floors, the store displays a large selection of kitchenware, tableware and accessories to accompany the collection. On the glass-fronted ground floor is a good choice of contemporary glassware and ceramics from the likes of iittala, Dartington Crystal and ASA ceramics, as well as selected accessories from a variety of companies and designers such as Alessi, Jasper Morrison and Nic Wood. The only furniture on sale is designed by Corin Mellor, David's son, well known for his understated yet sculptural bent-plywood tables and stools.The rather upbeat, contemporary atmosphere of the ground floor diminishes slightly in the basement, where there is an altogether more workaday array of kitchen utensils, pots, pans and crockery.

The friendly staff are informed ambassadors for Mellor's collection and will happily describe any detail of how these stainless-steel or silver-plated masterpieces are made. The classical music piped out around the store acts as a gentle reminder that you are among reputable, timeless British products of the highest quality and craftsmanship.

Mint
70 Wigmore Street
London W1U 2SF
020 7224 4406
Tube: Bond Street
Open: Mon – Sat 10:30 – 6:30
Thurs 11 – 7

Mint's unusual and eclectic array of interior goodies attracted considerable attention when owner Lina Kanafani launched the shop in December 1998. Bored of classics and labels, Lina wanted to sell an unexpected mix of objects that appealed to people with highly individual tastes.

Situated in a converted wine store, Mint has maintained many of the original features, such as the wonderful textural brickwork in the basement. The shop is quite small, but the two floors have been effectively designed, utilizing all available space without feeling cluttered.

Lina doesn't have preferences for particular designers or materials. Instead, she just sells what she loves best, though broadly speaking her style might be described as a blend of 'ethnic contemporary' and 'modern organic'. The tables, chairs, lights, rugs, blankets, cushions, vases, glasses and plates displayed here are sourced from all over the world.

Displays are ever-changing, as some pieces are one-offs or limited runs. A typical selection, though, might include ceramics by Jhan Stanley, modular tableware by Carine Tontini and Hub, and the elegant and curvaceous form of Guhl's concrete chair (pictured).

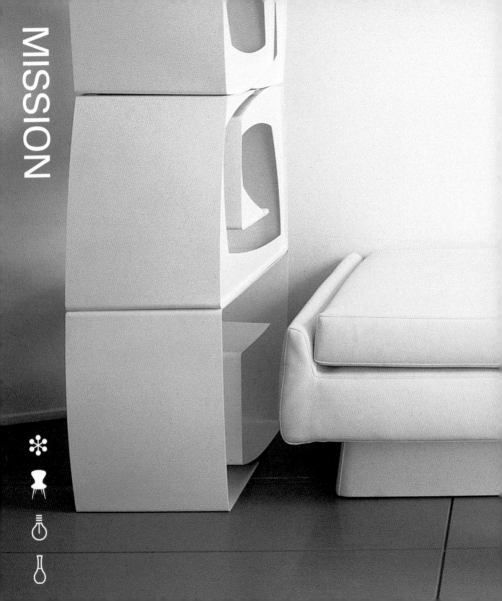

MISSION

Mission
45 Hereford Road
London W2 5AH
020 7792 4633
Tube: Notting Hill Gate or Bayswater
Open: Mon – Fri 11 – 6
Sat 1 – 4

Opened in May 1998 by design PR Yvonne Courtney and designer Misha Stefan, Mission aims to blur the boundaries between showspace, gallery and shop, with the furniture, lighting, ceramics, glass, books and accessories on offer complementing rather than dominating this uniquely calming space.

Periodically Mission stages exhibitions that showcase a particular style, era or area of expertise, but between shows it displays a highly personal choice of pieces designed by a wide variety of both young and established designers. At the time of my visit, Nelson's organic lighting forms (see pp. 234 – 35),

Patrick Fredrikson's graphic coat rack, Barnaby Tuke's elegant, crisp furniture, Ou Baholydhin's sharp stainless-steel accessories (see pp. 84 – 85) and Geraldine McGloin's interconnecting ceramics (see pp. 232 – 33) were gracing the space. Cubist wall pieces by Melanie Trievnor and 'soft geometric' furniture and lighting by Misha Stefan and Michael Wolfson (pictured) were particularly alluring in this gallery-like setting.

Mission's aim is to 'nurture the senses', challenging our definitions of retail spaces and setting new standards extending 'beyond the constraints of time'. This might seem rather intimidating, but both Yvonne and Misha provide a warm welcome and will provide more than enough expertise to leave you feeling inspired. Go and see for yourself!

Muji
Stores across London
and nationwide
Call 020 7323 2208 for
branches and opening hours

Well-known 'no-brand' retail company Muji opened its first shop in Japan in 1983. Its huge success in its native country rapidly led to expansion worldwide, including 15 stores in the UK alone. The company's four guiding principles, 'Good Value for Money', 'Simple and Functional Design', 'Basic and Understated Colour' and a 'Complete Lifestyle Product Range', create an image that is instantly recognizable and which happens to correspond closely to Western notions about Japanese minimalist design – clean, unfussy, functional. This pared-down aesthetic, combined with easily affordable price tags, is the key to the Muji phenomenon.

Selling furniture, storage, kitchenware, stationery, health and beauty products, and clothing, Muji stores offer a whole lifestyle package that successfully appeals to the 'one-stop' shopper. Expect no bold statements here. Slick stainless-steel kitchenware, elegant ceramics and semi-transparent polypropylene stationery are instant modern classics, combining muted colour and purity of form, without appearing overly 'designed'.

Functional and durable, the Muji product range looks set to outlive the fickleness of changing fashions that can so quickly date other mass-produced 'designer' goods.

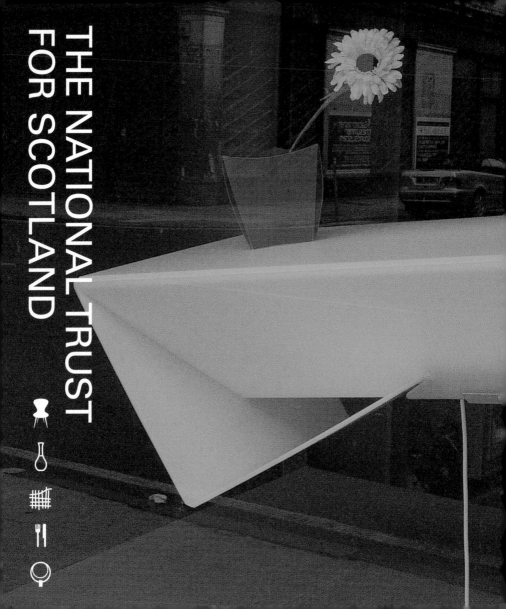

THE NATIONAL TRUST
FOR SCOTLAND

The National Trust for Scotland
Hutchesons' Hall
158 Ingram Street
Glasgow G1 1EJ
0141 552 8391
Open: Mon – Sat 10 – 5

Your image of National Trust shops is most likely to be one of day trippers purring over flowery tea towels and heritage coffee mugs with kittens on. If I'm wrong, then you have obviously already seen the revolutionary change that has occurred at Glasgow's Hutchesons' Hall.

Wanting to exploit the wealth of creative talent available in Glasgow, the National Trust for Scotland has dived headlong into the world of contemporary design. The Grade A–listed Hall has been transformed by award-winning Gareth Hoskins Architects into a comfortable yet avant-garde blend of classic and cutting edge. In a room that retains its original wooden panelling, glowing glass columns house an excellent selection of contemporary tableware, jewellery, bags and other accessories by designers such as Fireworks (see pp. 218 – 19), DNA (textiles), MK Design (ceramics), Arkitype (clocks) and Jan Milne (textiles). The pièce de résistance, however, is a ribbon-like, silver-painted plywood form that snakes around the space, housing the television screens and projectors that are used for installations.

It's immensely exciting and reassuring to find such an imaginative and innovative project realized, not by a young, designer-led company, but by a well-established organization like the National Trust. It's also an achievement that reflects the generally healthy state of contemporary design, at long last occupying the mainstream rather than confined to an elitist fringe.

OGGETTI

Oggetti
143 Fulham Road
London SW3 6SD
020 7581 8088
Tube: South Kensington
Open: Mon – Sat 9:30 – 6
Sun 12 – 5

If you are someone who likes to entertain your friends at home in style, then it's worth making a special journey to this stylish Fulham Road kitchen and tableware shop. Oggetti sells a selection of cutlery, crockery, and kitchen and tableware from around the world that is so astonishingly beautiful you are reminded just how attractive everyday objects can be. Alvar Aalto, Achille Castiglioni, Arne Jacobsen, Enzo Mari, Ferdinand Porsche, Ettore Sottsass and Tapio Wirkkala are the big names here. What caught my attention were oil and vinegar bottles designed by Enzo Mari (pictured) – if these don't improve your table settings, then nothing will! The shop also offers an impressive collection of unique Murano glass vases and platters, together with limited edition pewter tabletop centre pieces designed by Ettore Sottsass.

The shop interior is predominantly black, with the objects displayed in glowing white display cases, as if they were in a museum. Oggetti's helpful staff are design trained and able to give highly qualified advice. Pieces of such high quality are bound to be expensive, but you probably wouldn't have expected otherwise in this decidedly upmarket area of town.

Ogier
177 Westbourne Grove
London W11 2SB
020 7229 0783
ogier@dircon.co.uk
Tube: Notting Hill Gate
Open: Mon – Sat 11 – 6

Launched in September 1999 on Notting Hill's fashionable Westbourne Grove, Ogier dares to be different. In a generally Western-oriented design culture, owners Yves Ogier and Niki Frei wanted to add a twist of cutting-edge Asian style, offering a subtle fusion of new and old and East and West.

The designers here are a real mixed bag, although they are clearly carefully selected rather than simply herded together on grounds of commercial popularity or name. Lighting and accessories are designed by a handful of international young designers, such as New York-based design duo Studio 212, whose offerings here include various lights (pictured), tables and shelves that use materials such as aluminium, Perspex and leather. Other highlights include Andrew Tye's slick wooden furniture and partitions, Karin Schosser's porcelain artworks, Laurence Brabant's chunky crystal glasses, Christen Biecker's refined, clean-lined coffee tables, Sharon Marston's hairy lights and Michael Chung's Zen-like glowing side lights.

Ogier's collection, while eclectic and innovative, can cater for everyone's budgets, and is an excellent source for a stylish, unusual gift. The owners are often on site, so enthusiasm, advice and a warm welcome are all near-guaranteed.

OVERDOSE ON DESIGN

Overdose On Design
182 Brick Lane
London E1 6SP
020 7613 1266
www.overdoseondesign.com
Tube: Aldgate East or Liverpool Street
Open: Daily 11–6

This furniture emporium on the East End's bustling Brick Lane benefits from its prominent corner location and has certainly attracted a lot of attention since it first opened in 1999, quickly establishing a reputation for itself as a source of furniture and lighting originals dating roughly from 1945 to 1980. OOD's three rooms are packed with all manner of pieces by all sorts of designers, including Panton, Eames, Jacobsen, Le Corbusier, Mies van der Rohe, Colombo, Perriand, Bertoia, Wegner and Saarinen. With so much on offer and still more in storage, it's easy to see why many pieces are hired out for film and video shoots. The shop itself, however, is less than inspiring, with little thought given either to presentation or to the logistics of space and movement. Perhaps, though, this is a deliberate ploy, helping the shop to blend in with the area's other bric-a-brac-style shops. In any case, it's quite refreshing to find a shop dealing in the expensive world of mid-century modernism without the usual precious and pretentious trappings.

DESIGNERS INCLUDE:
Harry Bertoia
Joe Colombo
Le Corbusier
Charles and Ray Eames
Arne Jacobsen
Ludwig Mies van der Rohe
Verner Panton
Charlotte Perriand
Eero Saarinen
Hans Wegner

CHARLES PAGE

Charles Page
61 Fairfax Road
London NW6 4EE
020 7328 9851
www.charlespage.co.uk
info@charlespage.co.uk
Tube: Swiss Cottage
Open: Mon – Sat 9:30 – 5:30

Furniture retailer Charles Page originally opened this Swiss Cottage shop in 1921, selling pieces of a more traditional style. Today owned by a large company, the shop still retains both its old name and much of its old identity, capitalizing on its founder's reputation. The present Charles Page shop has considerably updated its image, however, and the spacious showroom stocks a choice of the understated, slick products you might expect to find from Italian giants such as Molteni, Minotti, Rimadesio (pictured), Maxalto and B&B Italia. Lighting is also available, with a selection of designs from Arco, Flos and Fontana Arte. Morrison's 'Globall' and Castiglioni's 'Arco' floorlight provide an eye-catching focus for what is an otherwise quite anonymous space.

Charles Page also designs and manufactures its own pieces. Enthusiastic interior designers Davied Patterson, Andrea Stothard and Andy Cliffe are available to help you materialize your ideas, be it a simple coffee table or a complete interior project.

In its advertising, Charles Page confidently declares itself to be 'one of Europe's best furniture shops'. This might be overstating the case, but if your taste is for good-quality, slightly conservative design, then Charles Page is undoubtedly an excellent bet.

PLACES AND SPACES

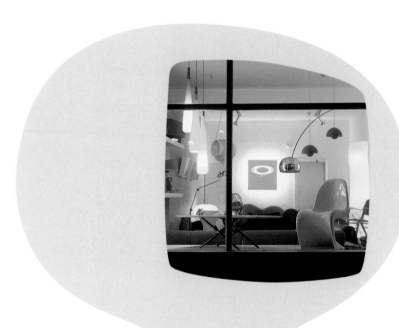

Places and Spaces
30 Old Town
London SW4 0LB
020 7498 0998
www.placesandspaces.com
contact@placesandspaces.com
Tube: Clapham Common
Open: Tues – Sat 10:30 – 6
Sun 12 – 4

Approaching this glowing, glass-fronted shopfront in the rather grey environs of Clapham's Old Town is bound to fill you with an almost childlike enthusiasm and glee. The philosophy of owners Paul Carroll and Nick Hannam is clearly 'Sell what you love best', and it's an idea that certainly works, since turnover of pieces is high. The appearance of the shop is constantly changing as pieces come and go, but expect an invigorating blend of classic and contemporary. Seating from the likes of Paulin, Panton, Eames and Wegner is successfully displayed alongside innovative lighting and accessories from such names as Nelson (see pp. 234 – 35), Sperlein (see pp. 240 – 41), Sponge (see pp. 242 – 43) and Sodeau. Considering the size of the shop, the range of furniture, lighting, ceramics, glass, artwork and accessories on display is impressively diverse.

If you are looking for a particular piece, it is recommended that you call in advance to check availability. Otherwise, just pop in for a burst of inspiration and a friendly chat with the helpful owners.

PLANET BAZAAR

DESIGNERS INCLUDE:
Alvar Aalto
Harry Bertoia
Charles and Ray Eames
Guzzini
Murano
Verner Panton
Pierre Paulin

Planet Bazaar
149 Drummond Street
London NW1 2PB
020 7387 8326
www.planetbazaar.co.uk
maureen@planetbazaar.demon.co.uk
Tube: Warren Street or Euston Square
Open: Tues – Sat 11:30 – 7
or by appointment

Maureen Silverman has been enthusiastically selling '50s to 80s designer furniture, art, glass, lighting, ceramics, books and eccentricities' since first opening this shop in the late 1990s. All of her stock consists of highly original and quirky design pieces sourced from various fairs around Europe, so there is no way of knowing what will be on display at any one particular time. On my visit, there were chairs by Panton, Eames, Paulin, Bertoia and Aalto as well as a selection of Murano glassware and 1970s Guzzini lighting. Guaranteed, however, is an excitingly unpredictable and eclectic array of designers, both known and unknown.

Surprise is the name of the game here, so call in advance if you are after something specific; otherwise, just pop in and you may snap up something unexpected or even rare – you never know what you might find.

Pop UK
17 High Street
Wimbledon Village
London SW19 5DX
020 8946 1122
www.popuk.com
Tube: Wimbledon
Open: Mon – Sat 10 – 6
Sun 12 – 5

41 – 43 Brighton Road
Croydon
Surrey CR2 6EB
020 8760 9660
Train: South Croydon
Open: As above

Brothers Auday and Richard Tokatly opened their first store in Croydon, where they exhibit an impressively diverse collection of contemporary furniture, lighting and accessories. Promoted as the last stop before Brighton for modern desirables, this spacious showroom continues to flourish. In 2000, however, the brothers opened a second, smaller shop in Wimbledon Village, where they now showcase the best of the Croydon branch's design offerings.

The Wimbledon shop stands out impressively on the rather smart and busy High Street. Benefiting from plenty of natural light and crisp white walls, the store has a fresh, up-beat feel and, although not particularly big, manages to offer an intelligent and generous choice that achieves a good balance between established and newer names. Well-known designers such as Ron Arad, Tom Dixon, Philippe Starck, Verner Panton, Arne Jacobsen and Michael Young share equal space and emphasis with the likes of up-and-coming talent such as Sponge (see pp.242 – 43), Ella Doran (see pp. 214 – 15), Karim Rashid, Michael Sodeau, Jam, Georgina Scott and thisisit.

Presentation has been carefully considered, and although there is plenty on offer, the shop avoids clutter. One or other of the friendly owners is normally in the store, so their enthusiasm and knowledge will be at your disposal in helping you choose what is right for you and your interior.

PREGO

Prego
Arch 17 North Quay
Victoria Quays
Sheffield S2 5SY
0114 275 5512
Open: Tues – Fri 10 – 6
Sat 10 – 5, Sun 11 – 4

Sheffield is home to one of the best contemporary furniture, lighting and accessories shops outside London. Situated in one of the beautifully converted canal-side storage chambers in Victoria Quays, Prego stocks a comprehensive mixture of furniture ranging from 20th-century classics by Eames, Le Corbusier and Mies van der Rohe to more recent designs by the likes of Matthew Hilton, Philippe Starck, Andrew Stafford and Terence Woodgate. As with many shops, Prego simply doesn't have enough space to display all its offerings, so customers are encouraged to peruse the many product portfolios for the complete range.

Especially well-represented are the larger producers, such as SCP (see pp. 168–169), Kartell, Magis, Alivar, Insitu, Driade, MDF Italia, Pallucco, Cassina, Vitra (see pp. 192–93) and Cappellini. With lighting ranging from beautifully hand-blown Italian glass pieces by Murano Due to the high-tech designs of Flos and Artemide, as well as a large selection of ceramics, glassware and pewterware, it's hard to go wrong here if you are looking to 'go modern'.

The owners are very approachable and are happy to spend time helping you make the right choice. Additional bonuses include wedding-list, contract-furniture and commissioning services.

PURE LIVING

Pure Living
1–3 Leonard Street
London EC2A 4AQ
020 7250 1116
mail@puredesignuk.com
Tube: Old Street
Open: Mon–Fri 10–6:30

Pure Living is an inspiring space, its two large and airy floors providing an impressive backdrop for the innovative design pieces on display. Interior designer Orianna Fielding Banks set up the showroom in March 1999 with the intention of showing the work of today's new designers and artists in a stimulating, 'melting-pot' environment that, in her words, responds to the 'shifting nature of today's urban lifestyle'. Running a full interior-design service from the offices at the rear, Fielding Banks offers not only a highly desirable shop-floor collection featuring furniture, lighting, accessories and artwork from some of the UK's most forward-thinking and imaginative designers but also a full commissioning service.

The range and quality of designs is exceptional. Fluorescent 'Rocking Bean' chairs by Sponge (see pp. 242–43), the multifunctional configuration of Fiona Davidson's 'Room Project 1' (see pp. 210–11) and mesmerizing, glittering wall pieces by Design Elements sit alongside Kode Tokyou's lights, Kathy Dalwood's ceramics, WW.Modcons' accessories (see pp. 248–49), Ferrious' 'Eight Fifty' floorlights (see pp. 80–81), Happell's interactive coffee table (see pp. 222–23), Yoma London's cushions, Kate Maestri's glassworks, and thisisit's warped metal platters. Artworks also adorn the walls, with pieces by Baljit Balrow and Geoff Linney hung beside the colourful, abstract photography of Michael Banks.

Exposed brick walls, concrete floors and original wooden beams combine with a remarkably open feel to give the shop a gallery-like ambience, though without the usual gallery-style pretentiousness. The staff are friendly and enthusiastic, helping to make a visit to this store a uniquely uplifting experience.

PURVES & PURVES

Purves & Purves
220 – 224 Tottenham Court Road
London W1P 9HD
020 7580 8223
www.purves.co.uk
Tube: Goodge Street
Open: Mon – Sat 9:30 – 6
Except Tues 10 – 6 & Thurs 9:30 – 7:30

Contemporary design emporium Purves & Purves was opened by Andrew and Pauline Purves on Central London's busy Tottenham Court Road in 1992. The duo were brave enough to introduce innovative work to a broader public at a time when the general attitude towards 'cutting-edge' design was still rather backward and when the recession was still biting deep into people's pockets. Fortunately reactions to the project were positive and, with the restoration of consumer confidence in the mid-1990s, the store began to prosper and was able to expand its product selection to the impressive size it offers today. Purves & Purves has recently moved to larger premises half way up Tottenham Court Road where it will benefit from plenty of passing trade.

The big European manufacturers dominate, with a seemingly infinite array of sofas, chairs, tables and stools from the likes of B&B Italia, Hitch Mylius, Magis, Kartell, XO, Driade and COR. Furniture covers most of the two floors, with lighting restricted to a corner area that displays designs by Foscarini, Fontana Arte, Flos, Luceplan and De Majo. Besides the star names, however, the owners are also keen to support independent designers, and scattered around the shop you will find pieces by less well-known designers such as Anthony Dickens (see pp. 212 – 13), Ella Doran (see pp. 214 – 15), Sponge (see pp. 242 – 243), El Ultimo Grito (see pp. 244 – 245), Lynne Wilson (see pp. 246 – 247) and Gecko. Previously a little intimidating, the new Purves & Purves certainly seems more inviting with a café at the back to rest one's over-shopped feet! The accessories section, selling an array of kitchenware, tableware, ceramics and glass from names such as Alessi, Authentics, ASA, Zack, Umbra and Benetton, is normally bustling.

Purves & Purves should certainly be commended for its bold showcasing of contemporary items. Its success has made the store a well-known name and, with a significant presence in the West End of London and a shop in Canary Wharf, it looks set to grow.

Retro Home
20 Pembridge Road
London W11 3HL
020 7221 2055
www.buy-sell-trade.co.uk
Tube: Notting Hill Gate
Open: Daily 10 – 8

Retro Home is just one of the 18 shops that make up the chain of 'Buy! Sell! Trade!' General Trading Stores. Each of the shops specializes in a particular retail area, such as music and videos, books, computers or clothing, but all are unusual in that it is the public that provides the stock, bringing in articles to exchange or sell.

As its name implies, Retro Home's speciality is 20th-century furnishings and objets d'art. As the store relies on whatever turns up, there is no knowing what the shop will look like on each visit.

Nor is there a bias towards any particular period or style, so a display cabinet might contain 1950s or 1960s kitsch plastics sitting alongside elegant Holmegaard glassware.

This small shop has two floors. On the ground floor during my visit were Hornsea, Denby, Poole, Arabia and Portmeirion ceramics and Whitefriars, Orrefors, Murano and Baccarat glassware, as well as a jumble of toys, lighting, clocks, telephones and artworks. Downstairs in the rather gloomy basement were pieces by Panton, Eames, Bertoia (pictured), Day, Colombo, Aalto and Sottsass, all rather haphazardly but democratically displayed alongside retro unknowns.

Surprisingly for Notting Hill, this shop has few pretensions, making a visit here really quite a pleasure. There may be one or two treasures in store, so take the time to scour.

ROOST

Roost
26 Kensington Gardens
Brighton BN1 4AL
01273 625 223
Open: Mon – Fri 10 – 5:30
Sat 10 – 6, Sun 12 – 4:30

Amid the hustle and bustle of Brighton's pedestrianized Kensington Gardens sits furniture, lighting, glassware, ceramics and accessories shop Roost. Opened in the late 1990s by Lucien Hewetson and Claire Gilliver, this small shop has certainly evolved into a place to know about. 'Affordable contemporary' is the thing here, making for a wonderful combination of unpredictable accessories and innovative yet sensible furniture that won't break the bank.

The owners have fully realized the importance of remaining interesting, fresh and affordable in order to appeal to Brighton's design-hungry consumers. Ceramics by Brighton-based talents Hub (see pp. 226 – 27) and Marc Boase (see pp. 204 – 205), woven-cane lights by Michael Sodeau, seating by David Design, lighting by Peter Wylly of Babylon (see pp. 32 – 33) and Proto Design, and hand-made ceramics by London-based Julie Goodwin and Karen Smith (pictured), are just some of the products on offer here. Individual, original and affordable, Roost has certainly found a winning formula.

ROUND THE WORLD

Round the World
15 North West Circus Place
Edinburgh EH3 6SX
0131 225 7800
www.rtw-uk.com
info@rtw-uk.com
Open: Mon – Sat 10 – 6

Round the World's owners, Michael and Susan Gordon, opened their shop in a converted bank in Edinburgh's New Town in 1997. Having moved in, they decided to keep some of the bank's original features, including the handsome marble flooring, leather banquettes and wooden panelling, providing the shop with a uniquely striking edge. Best of all, the handsome cashiers' desk close to the entrance has been turned into a bar serving gourmet coffee (pictured), providing customers with a space to mull over just what they are going to buy from this excellent, well-stocked shop.

Round the World is made up of a number of rooms spread over two floors, including a small basement space. There is a huge selection of furniture, lighting, storage and accessories, with most of the big names available, including B&B Italia, lapalma, Kartell, MDF Italia, XO, SCP see pp.168 – 69), Magis and Flos. Towards the front of the shop are accessories, with a large array of glass and tableware on offer from star names such as LSA International, Authentics, Alessi and Zack.

Product portfolios complete the available ranges, while an interior-design service is ready to take the strain out of furnishing your house. And even if you do find the whole thing overwhelming, remember there's always the café to resort to!

SCP
135 – 139 Curtain Road
London EC2A 3BX
020 7739 1869
www.scp.co.uk
scp@scp.co.uk
Tube: Old Street
Open: Mon – Sat 9:30 – 6

Before opening SCP in 1985, Sheridan Coakley was involved in the manufacture of tubular-steel furniture and the importation of Italian re-editions of classic pieces by Mies van der Rohe and Le Corbusier. An encounter with the contemporary furniture of Philippe Starck in Paris also led him to become the first UK importer of this now seminal designer's work.

Over the last 15 years, Coakley has developed close working partnerships with a number of top British designers, manufacturing pieces by Jasper Morrison, Matthew Hilton and Terence Woodgate among many others. He has been a key player in establishing many talented young designers, turning some into internationally recognized icons of contemporary design.

SCP's large, intelligently arranged retail space in what is now ultra-fashionable Shoreditch is spread over two floors, offering a perfect fusion of both classic and contemporary pieces that never feels forced. The arrangement of products has evidently been carefully thought out, balancing spaciousness with excellent product choice. Glassware from iittala and Wagenfeld, tableware from Gropius, cutlery from Hackman and furniture from Morrison, Woodgate, Hilton, Whiteread (pictured), Starck, One Foot Taller (see pp. 236 – 37), Stafford, Marriott, Irvine, Grcic, Dixon, Jacobsen, Gray, Paulin, Eames, Le Corbusier, Kjaerholm, Panton, Breuer, Yanagi, Mies van der Rohe, Aalto, Noguchi, Bertoia, Hoffmann, Saarinen… the list is every design-lover's dream. SCP also has a concession in Selfridges (4th Floor, 400 Oxford Street, London W1A 1AB; tel 020 7318 3138), helping to give this famous department store a more contemporary feel (pictured below).

SCP's Shoreditch shop has left a lasting impression on me, and I hope it has the same effect on you!

SHANNON

Shannon
68 Walcot Street
Bath BA1 5BD
01225 424 222
www.shannonuk.com
sales@shannonuk.com
Open: Mon – Sat 9:30 – 5:30

Strolling along a street dominated by antique dealers and salvage shops, I was both surprised and relieved to find Sue Shannon's recently opened furniture, lighting and accessories shop, which specializes in the elegant designs of the great 20th-century Scandinavian masters as well as contemporary pieces from the region.

Having been drawn into this oasis of fluid forms and clean simplicity, I was greeted by Hans Wegner's finely crafted wooden furniture, the refined elegance of Poul Kjaerholm's PK furniture series and Bruno Mathasson's luxurious bent-plywood and hemp-webbed chairs. Further in, I was entranced by a selection of lights designed by Denmark's Pandul and Le Klint. Accessories were also well represented, including glass from iittala, Hadeland and Lindshammar, ceramics by Arabia and Arne Jacobsen's stainless-steel wonders for Stelton. A variety of clocks, mirrors and pottery, crafted either locally or elsewhere in Europe, complete this beautiful collection.

The coupling of such classic offerings with the friendly service create an overall look and feel that is warm, comfortable and relaxed. In a city that sometimes feels as if it is stuck in the past, Shannon is a beacon of progressive contemporaneity.

SKANDIUM

Skandium
72 Wigmore Street
London W1H 9DL
020 7935 2077
www.skandium.com
skandium@skandium.com
Tube: Bond Street
Open: Mon – Sat 10 – 6:30
Sun 12 – 5

The Scandinavians are renowned for their attention to detail, with quality, refinement and pleasing aesthetics all sustained at the highest level in their designs. Such masters as Panton, Jacobsen, Aalto, Henningsen, Wegner and Kjaerholm have all produced pieces that have received worldwide recognition, placing the Scandinavian countries at the forefront of contemporary design. Skandium seeks to build on this reputation. Jointly owned by a Swede, a Finn and a Dane, the shop has been open only since September 1999. In just a short time, however, this light and airy space, with its 3.5-metre-high curved pine wall, painted wooden and glass floors, and slick product presentation, has established itself firmly on the London design scene.

Skandium is a lifestyle shop, selling a perfectly selected blend of classic and contemporary Scandinavian furniture, lighting, glass, china, rugs, fabrics, books and other accessories. Furniture classics from the great masters mentioned above combine well with designs by Scandinavia's new generation of talents, including David Design, Harri Koskinen, architect Thomas Sandell and trio Claesson, Koivisto and Rune. iittala glass, Stelton stainless-steel kitchenware, Vola bathroom fittings, Hackman cutlery, Arabia tableware and Kinnasand and Marimekko geometric fabrics are all sure to leave you breathless with desire, and the good-looking, friendly and knowledgeable staff will do all they can to help you make the right choice.

DESIGNERS INCLUDE:
Jonathan Adler
Bowles and Linares
Sophie Cook
Ceci LePage
Theo Williams

Space
214 Westbourne Grove
London W11 2RH
020 7229 6533
www.spaceshop.co.uk
boudoir@spaceshop.co.uk
Tube: Notting Hill Gate
Open: Mon – Sat 10 – 6

Emma Oldham launched the new-look Space in September 1999, unveiling a new collection of sensual bed linens and lifestyle luxuries under the name Space Boudoir. According to Oldham, the range is about mixing 'the beautiful with the desirable, the more affordable with the aspirational'. The bed-linen collection oozes glamour and sensuality, with silk and satin eiderdowns and jewel-clustered pashmina dressing gowns among just some of the luxuries on offer. Hand-embroidered detailing adds a touch of old-fashioned class.

In addition to the bed linen, there is a beautiful selection of carefully sourced products, including black Vietnamese lacquerware, Jonathan Adler's vases from New York, awe-inspiring acrylic vases from LePage (pictured) and Theo Williams' clean-lined furniture. Bowles & Linares' (see pp. 36–37) hand-blown glass cafetières and Sophie Cook's ceramic vases are reassuring additions – a reminder that quality, handmade work is still valued in a world obsessed with the mass-produced.

Space is devoted to the finer things of life and as such certainly deserves a visit. For those sybarites too slothful to make their way to Westbourne Grove, there is an excellent mail-order service.

SUBURBIA

Suburbia
17 Regent Street
Clifton
Bristol
BS8 4HW
0117 974 3880
Open: Mon 1 – 6
Tues – Sat 10 – 6

Sue Williams opened this understated shop in picturesque Clifton in October 1999, having spotted Bristol's largely unsatisfied demand for contemporary design. With its cool, grey walls and overall fresh, clean image, the shop has an unusual feeling of exclusivity, but without the prices to match – nothing costs more than about £200, with most products coming in at around £10 to £50. Body-moulding beanbags from Inflate, elegant glassware from LSA International and organic-shaped ceramics by Michael Sodeau are just some of the pieces available in this small space. A good selection of art and design books and magazines is also available.

Williams is keen to support new design work, and as part of her launch she commissioned local designer Johnno Farrar to produce a range of bowls and platters in his signature material, concrete, and these, apparently, are selling extremely well. William's success is promising and should give heart to other entrepreneurs considering setting up a design store out of London.

DESIGNERS INCLUDE:
Aero
Johnno Farrar
Inflate
LSA International
Michael Sodeau

TANGRAM

Tangram
33/37 Jeffrey Street
Edinburgh
EH1 1DH
0131 556 6551
www.tangramfurnishers.co.uk
Open: Tues – Fri 10 – 5:30
Sat 10 – 5

Eleanor and Julian Darwell-Stone's shop has been supplying furniture, lighting, textiles and rugs to the contract and domestic markets since 1994. In February 2000, however, Tangram moved to larger premises just up the hill from Edinburgh's mainline station.

The shop's high-quality selection combines clean, modern forms with understated yet innovative detailing. Selling big names such as B&B Italia (pictured), Baleri Italia, Lammhults and Montis, it also provides more exclusive offerings from furniture manufacturers Piiroinen Arena, Amat, Stua, Horm and Mobles 114. Products are extremely well displayed, free from the clutter that so often spoils shops with similarly large product portfolios. Tangram's owners, it seems, understand the importance of allowing every piece the space to breathe, giving prospective buyers the opportunity to view objects untrammelled. Unfortunately there's no interior-design service, but the helpful staff are ready to give knowledgeable advice on every option open to you. An excellent website showcases the majority of the available products and will inspire you while hunting for that perfect interior look.

Themes & Variations
231 Westbourne Grove
London W11 2SE
020 7727 5531
Tube: Notting Hill Gate
Open: Mon – Fri 10 – 1 & 2 – 6
Sat 10 – 6

Themes & Variations first opened its doors in 1985, before Westbourne Grove had become quite so well known and fashionable as it is today. Selling an eclectic and careful selection of 1950s, 60s and 70s Scandinavian design as well as a range of contemporary European pieces, this beautiful gallery-like space exudes exclusivity.

The furniture, lighting, glassware and jewellery on display eschew any indication of mass-production for a stylistic individualism that is unlikely to be universally appealing. Original glass vases by Tapio Wirkkala for iittala sit elegantly on ornate revived Fornasetti furniture; Tom Dixon's 'Spiral' light towers stand next to a 'Samurai' pleated-paper light by Ingo Maurer.

With the one-off feel of many of the products and its lucid, uncluttered presentation, Themes & Variations runs the risk of seeming intimidating. However, the provocative, love-or-hate nature of many of the pieces make this shop a unique experience.

TOM TOM

DESIGNERS INCLUDE:
Harry Bertoia
Charles and Ray Eames
Arne Jacobsen
Ingo Maurer
Verner Panton

Tom Tom
42 New Compton Street
London WC2H 8DA
020 7240 7909
www.tomtomshop.co.uk
Tube: Tottenham Court Road
Open: Tues – Fri 12 – 7
Sat 11 – 6 or by appointment

Tom Tom's charismatic owner, Tommy Roberts, opened his shop in 1995 in a quiet yet centrally located street between Charing Cross Road and Shaftesbury Avenue. Selling post-war, retro furniture, lighting and accessories, Roberts refers to the design classics in which the shop specializes as antiques because everything is original with no present-day reproductions on offer. Packed into the two floors of this small space at the time of my visit were some well-known pieces by the ever-popular Eameses, Jacobsen, Maurer, Bertoia and Panton.

Be warned, however: owing to the shop's band of loyal followers, turnover of these desirables is fast. If you are after something specific, it's probably a good idea to telephone in advance. Even if that special something is unavailable, Tommy's knowledge and sourcing abilities may work wonders, though you may have to be a little patient.

TWENTYTWENTYONE

twentytwentyone
274 Upper Street
London N1 2UA
020 7288 1996
www.twentytwentyone.com
mail@twentytwentyone.com
Tube: Angel or Highbury & Islington
Open: Mon – Fri 10 – 6
Sat 10 – 5:30

In 1993 Simon Alderson and Tony Cunningham formed a partnership called 'twentieth century design', selling original modern furniture, lighting and industrial design from a converted stable in Camden Town. In 1996 the duo went on to open a retail space in Islington.

In 1998 the shop underwent a revamp, adding contemporary design to the mid-century staples, and changing its name accordingly to 'twentytwentyone'. The fusion of 'classic' and 'cutting-edge' works well here, with dark woods, textured upholstery and clean, crisp ceramics creating a sharp yet warm overall look.

Furniture from Wegner, Eames, Bertoia, Day and Kjaerholm is elegantly displayed next to Michael Sodeau's woven-cane lights and Jessie Higginson's sharply defined ceramic vases. Accessories, including glassware from Royal Copenhagen or Michael Young's S.M.A.K jewellery, are shown in the beautiful glass display cases that line one wall of the shop. The floor-to-ceiling glass shopfront allows plenty of natural light to reach the rear of the shop, where most of the furniture is displayed. An extensive selection of design books make this gorgeous-looking shop a good place to find style-conscious friends an affordable but handsome gift.

A warehouse-like space selling a larger selection of pieces can be found at: 18c River Street, London EC1R 1XN (tel 020 7837 1900).

Utility
85 Bold Street
Liverpool L1 4HF
0151 707 9919
www.utilityretail.co.uk
Open: Mon – Sat 10 – 6

Since opening in November 1999, Utility has succeeded in appealing to Liverpool's design-conscious inhabitants, and has been able to benefit from a lot of passing trade on the city's busy Bold Street.

Selling mainly an array of smaller accessories such as clocks, mirrors, vases, glass, ceramics, watches and bathroom products, the owners are keen to introduce more furniture and lighting into their small premises. When I visited, I was pleasantly surprised to find work from the likes of Marc Boase (see pp. 204 – 205), Ella Doran (see pp. 214 – 15), Fireworks (see pp. 218 – 19), Hub (see pp. 226 – 27) and El Ultimo Grito

(see pp. 244–45), alongside Hackman cutlery, iittala and LSA International glassware, Keramica vases, Guzzini and Alessi kitchenware and Corin Mellor bent-plywood furniture (pictured).

Despite the range on offer, the shop somehow manages to avoid clutter, with the plentiful natural light that pours through the original Georgian shopfront adding to the feeling of airy spaciousness. The staff are fantastically enthusiastic about design and will happily talk about aspects of the work on offer if prompted. As Liverpool's city centre continues to regenerate, they are confident that increasing numbers of its inhabitants will become hooked on contemporary design.

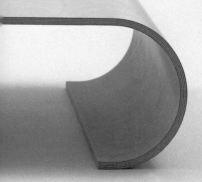

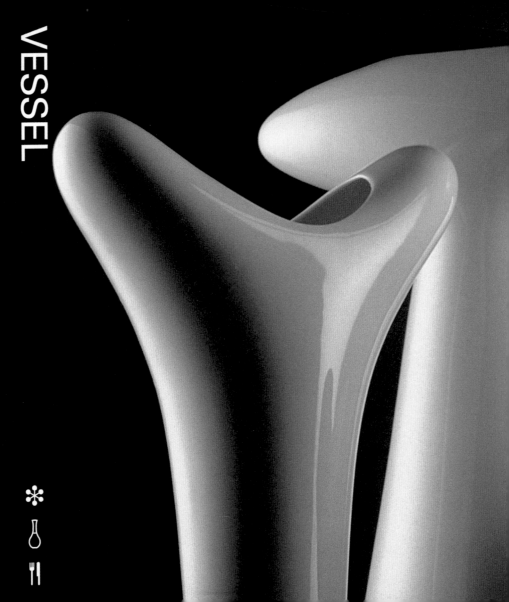

VESSEL

Vessel
114 Kensington Park Road
London W11 2PW
020 7727 8001
Tube: Notting Hill Gate
Open: Mon – Sat 10 – 6

In spring 1999 fashionable Notting Hill saw the opening of Vessel, the modern 'one-stop table accessory' mecca of contemporary glass- and ceramicware.

Owner Nadia Demetriou Ladas and Angel Monzón are tremendously passionate about what they sell and source products from around the world, with their prime criteria comprising 'beauty, quality, function and affordability'. Their passion comes across in the shop, where each and every piece is exhibited with care and consideration.

Vessel's strength lies in its exclusive focus on tableware. Nadia and Angela are keen to find the classics of tomorrow and are constantly looking for new talents to showcase. Combining the work of new pioneers such as Marc Boase (see pp. 204 – 205), Amy Cushing (see pp. 208 – 209), Caterina Fadda (see pp. 216 – 17), Bodo Sperlein (see pp. 240 – 41), Karine Smith, Brian Keaney, Rachel Urbicki, Rina Menardi,

Karin Schosser (pictured) and Sheila Hay with that of more established names such as Hackman, Arabia, iittala, Stelton, Rosenthal, Salviati, Simon Moore, Orrefors, Driade and Arcade, Vessel offers a wealth of choice to customers looking for something beautiful in addition to pure functionality.

Everything on display is individual and about as far as can be from the mundane fare of high-street shops. This serene and understated shop, beautifully designed by Angel Monzón, is a pure delight.

VIADUCT

DESIGNERS INCLUDE:
Driade
MDF Italia
Montis
Pallucco
Maarten van Severen
XO
Zeus

Viaduct
1 – 10 Summer's Street
London EC1R 5BD
020 7278 8456
www.viaduct.co.uk
info@viaduct.co.uk
Tube: Chancery Lane or Farringdon
Open: Mon – Fri 9:30 – 6
Sat 10:30 – 4

Viaduct, I had been told, was more of a showroom than a shop, so it was with some trepidation that I paid a visit to this City furniture emporium. I needn't have worried because the staff actually give a friendly welcome to the general public despite the shop's extensive involvement with the contract market. Situated in a huge, double-height converted warehouse space, Viaduct looks impressive both inside and out, largely thanks to its large, beautiful windows that allow plenty of natural light to flood onto the displays within.

Viaduct specializes in European design and, in addition to supplying pieces from a wide range of companies, is an agent for seven of the continent's most influential manufacturers – Driade, Maarten van Severen, MDF Italia, Montis, Pallucco, XO and Zeus. In case that means nothing to you, think Starck, Hilton, Grcic and Lovegrove. It's not until you see Viaduct's impressive library of product information, however, that you realize just what a comprehensive selection of furniture, lighting and accessories it provides.

It really requires a visit to Viaduct to grasp the full range of possibilities that are available here. Whether you are kitting out your place from scratch or just interested in expanding your design knowledge, make a trip to this showroom.

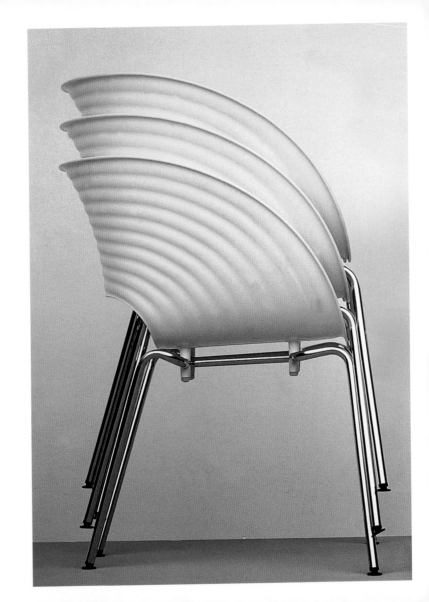

VITRA

Vitra
30 Clerkenwell Road
London EC1M 5PQ
020 7608 6200
www.vitra.com
info_uk@vitra.com
Tube: Barbican
Open: Mon – Sat 9 – 5:30
Sun 9 – 4:30

Founded in the 1950s, Vitra has grown to become one of the world's key players in the contemporary furniture-manufacturing market, putting into production designs from big names such as Panton, Eames, Morrison, Citterio, Starck, van Severen and Arad (pictured), among many others. Their support of contemporary design also continues into architecture, with factories, offices, a museum and even a fire station designed by architects of the standing of Nicholas Grimshaw, Frank Gehry, Tadao Ando and Zaha Hadid. The newest addition is the David Chipperfield-designed London showroom (pictured), which opened in September 1999. The massive new selling space occupies three floors in a converted Clerkenwell industrial building. Huge windows running along the front of the showroom flood the space with natural light, bringing the furniture display to life and reinforcing the Vitra slogan of 'good goods'. The range of domestic and contract seating and office furniture is immense, so a visit to this minimalist-design haven is highly recommended to get a feel for the 'comfortable, technologically outstanding, ergonomic, ecological, economical, and aesthetically attractive' products on offer.

WADE SMITH
APARTMENT STORE

DESIGNERS INCLUDE:
Alessi
Le Corbusier
Henry Dean
Designers Guild
Ella Doran
Hackman
Matthew Hilton
iittala
Inflate
LSA International
SCP
Siemens

Wade Smith Apartment Store
Matthew Street
Liverpool L2 6RE
0151 224 7617
www.wadesmith.co.uk
Open: Mon – Sat 9:30 – 5:30
Sun 12 – 4

A new venture for shoes and clothes retailer Wade Smith, this design 'department store' was launched to the Liverpudlian public at the end of March 2000 in the basement of its existing centrally located shop. At a time when 'loft-living' is becoming increasingly popular in the city, Wade Smith has clearly seen the potential of expanding into contemporary homewares.

The space is separated into 'departments' for the 'apartment', with different sections for lighting, glass, kitchens, furniture, bathrooms, bedrooms, gardens and accessories. Generally the shop sticks to the safer, bigger names, clearly not wanting to scare off wary consumers with anything too garish or avant-garde. Aiming to please everyone's budgets, Wade Smith stocks affordable glassware from LSA International, iittala and some of Henry Dean's handmade glass pieces, as well as more expensive furniture, such as Matthew Hilton's 'Balzac' chair and Le Corbusier's famous 'Chaise Longue'.

It's already encouraging to find names such as Hackman, Inflate, Ella Doran (see pp. 214 – 15), Designers Guild (see pp. 58 – 59), Siemens, Alessi (see pp. 16 – 17) and SCP (see pp. 168 – 69) shown here, but more exciting is the news that Wade Smith is considering introducing designs from local young talent. This would turn an already good shop into a pioneering northern design haven.

Whippet is the creation of Vincent Wainwright, who opened his first shop near Crystal Palace in 1997. Selling mainly home accessories, Wainwright has always been keen to avoid the usual giftshop jumble of characterless picture frames and tacky plastic gimmicks. Instead, he chooses a range of glass ceramics, candles, bathroom accessories, cards, cushions and some lighting and furniture that remains affordable while offering a touch more style. Wainright has both enthusiasm and flair, and he understands well the effect even a small object can have on a room. His formula has obviously worked because in March 2000 he opened his second shop, this time in East Sheen, between Richmond and Barnes. Featuring products from LSA International, ASA Ceramics, Hackman, Room, Inflate, Eurolounge, iittala, Arabia and Authentics, the selection is similar to the first shop, though perhaps slightly more upmarket.

If it's a gift you are looking for, then Whippet is an excellent place to start your search, with low to moderate budgets well catered for.

197

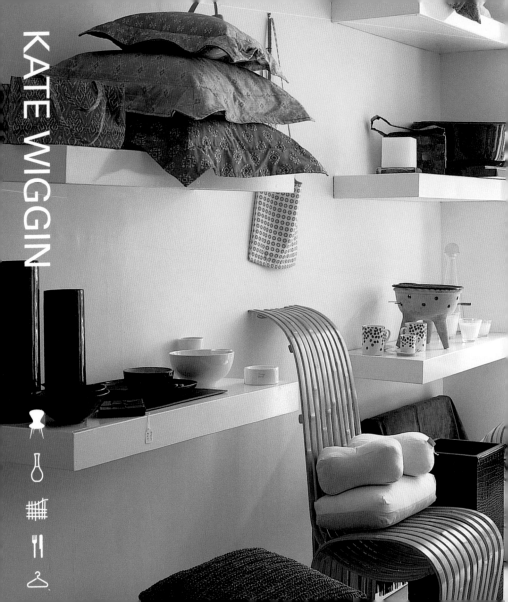

KATE WIGGIN

Kate Wiggin
The Lifestyle Shop
39 St Stephen Street
Edinburgh EH3 5AH
0131 225 2606
Open: Mon – Sat 10 – 6

Kate Wiggin opened her shop on calm, eclectic St Stephen Street in Edinburgh's New Town in September 1999. Despite limited space, the bubbly and enthusiastic owner has managed to pack in an impressive selection of tableware, accessories, artwork, clothes, shoes and bags, together with some pieces of furniture.

Having set herself the challenge of finding contemporary designs that harmonize with the traditional Scottish domestic style, she has placed the emphasis here on natural, sensuous, fabrics and materials, such as bamboo, leather, slate, stone, wood, ceramic, glass, wax and wool.

Leather accessories from Bill Amberg and Alma Home (see pp.18 – 19), ceramics from Nicola Tassie and Marc Boase (see pp. 204 – 205) and glassware from Broste and LSA International were among the striking products I found during my visit.

Kate Wiggin has gifts to suit any budget, although you will probably not be able to leave without having first bought something individual for yourself.

MARC BOASE ELLA DORAN L
SPONGE TOM KIRK CATERINA
GEORG BALDELE MAKÉ DESIG
ONE FOOT TALLER FIONA DAV
CARL CLERKIN AMY CUSHIN
EL ULTIMO GRITO NELSON W
ELLA DORAN CATERINA FADD
LYNNE WILSON GERALDINE M
MAKÉ DESIGN FIREWORKS B
ELLA DORAN GITTA GSCHWE
EL ULTIMO GRITO AMY CUSH
WW.MODCONS HIVE GERALD
MAX SHEPHERD GEORG BALD

NE WILSON MAX SHEPHERD
FADDA GERALDINE MCGLOIN
FIREWORKS BODO SPERLEIN
SON GITTA GSCHWENDTNER
MOSQUITO SPONGE NELSON
MODCONS ONE FOOT TALLER
HAPPELL ANTHONY DICKENS
GLOIN HUB GEORG BALDELE
O SPERLEIN **DESIGNERS** HIVE
TNER CARL CLERKIN NELSON
G.MOSQUITO LYNNE WILSON
E MCGLOIN FIONA DAVIDSON
E TOM KIRK BODO SPERLEIN

GEORG BALDELE

AWARDS
Blueprint/100% Design
Award Special Prize
(1998)

DESIGN EVENTS
Stealing Beauty, ICA,
London (1999)
Salone Satellite, with
RCA, Milan Furniture Fair,
Italy (April 1999)
Lost and Found,
The British Council,
International Touring
Exhibition (1999)
Designers Block, Brick
Lane, London (Sept 1999)
Fly Candle Fly
Installation, Saatchi
Gallery, London (2000)
Designers Block,
St Pancras Chambers,
London (Oct 2000)

UK RETAILERS
Contact Georg Baldele's
studio for stockists

Georg Baldele
The Dove Centre – Unit 15
109 Bartholomew Road
London NW5 2BJ
020 7482 2032
georg-baldele@yahoo.co.uk

Energetic and enthusiastic Austrian-born product designer Georg Baldele has had an impeccable training. A graduate in mechanical engineering, he went on to take a masters in product design in Vienna. It was here that he began work on 'Fly Candle Fly', a simple yet magically atmospheric product that reproduces the effect of a ghostly, floating candle by passing two virtually invisible heat-resistant wires through the length of a slow-burning candle and then hanging them from the ceiling. The work captured the eye of a visiting professor, none other than Ron Arad, who subsequently introduced Baldele and his work to the lighting maestro Ingo Maurer at the Milan Furniture Fair in 1996. Maurer, too, was impressed and financed 'Fly Candle Fly's' development. After some teething problems, the product was finally launched three years later at Milan, to great acclaim. The piece has been exhibited in installations in places as diverse as the Victoria and Albert Museum and the Saatchi Gallery.

After finishing his course in Vienna, Baldele went on to study furniture design at the Royal College of Art, from which he graduated in 1998. The simplicity and playfulness of his designs continued with the 'Caveman' series of paper lights. Huge coils of heat-resistant paper are pulled up from the centre, stiffened with resin glue and lit from within. These glowing pillars of creamy industrial paper can reach over two metres in height and are always totally unique, despite originating from a mass-produced material. While the hand-crafted, one-off appearance is a key attribute of the pieces, Baldele is currently looking for ways to make a mass-produced version.

A student competition for the Swedish company Perstorp inspired Baldele to design prototype flooring that flew in the face of the company's 15-year wear-and-tear guarantee. The flooring is made up of two thick layers of colour so that as the top surface is worn away, a second layer of colour is revealed, creating a 'user-unique' textural evolution. Georg has subsequently designed more subtle flooring for Pergo, which is available at Ikea.

Another ingenious design was 'Gonfi', a small inflatable pen that folds up and fits neatly into a pocket. Its inspiration was Baldele's own frustrating experience of always breaking the pens that – like any good designer – he stuck nonchalantly in his back pocket. 'Gonfi' pens can be branded with any logo, offering companies effective promotional opportunities.

Georg's interest in introducing touches of individualism to the blandness of mass-production will certainly continue to fuel his creativity and imagination, while his combination of innovation and commercial awareness will no doubt ensure his growing success.

MARC BOASE

Marc Boase
33 Lower Market Street
Brighton BN3 1AT
01273 328 603
07976 608 376
marcboase@pavilion.co.uk

AWARDS
Crafts Council/Elle
Decoration – 50%-off
stand at 100% Design
(Sept 1999)
Smeg /Living etc. Design
Competition winner
Ceramics/Glass
category (Oct 1999)

DESIGN EVENTS
Top Drawer, Earls Court,
London (1999)
Smeg/Living etc.
design competition,
London (Nov 1999)
Creative Britain
(British European
Design Group),
Frankfurt, Germany (2000)
100% Design,
Earls Court, London
(Oct 2000)

UK RETAILERS
Falconer, London
Graham & Green, London
Harrods, London
Kume, Brighton
Mint, London
Roost, Brighton
Utility, Liverpool
Vessel, London
Kate Wiggin, Edinburgh

Since graduating in 3-D design from the University of Brighton in 1997, Boase has created an innovative yet practical range of ceramic tableware and accessories. Although interested in a variety of materials, he quickly realized the commercial advantages of working with ceramics as an affordable starting point for a young, relatively unknown designer. Fortunately the initial struggle to find a suitable manufacturer is over, and as press and retail attention continues to grow, Boase can once again give his full attention to his product.

Boase's inspiration comes from experimenting with everyday shapes and forms. Function is important, too, however – 'Letting the function dictate the shape is how you keep the beauty of the object alive,' he says. Breaking away from traditional expectations of ceramics, his innovative range of vases, bowls, dishes, ashtrays, saucers and jugs remains simple, practical and unobtrusive.

His 'Shroom' vase, for example, sustains its beauty with or without flowers owing to its alluring organic form. His stand at 100% Design in October 2000 saw the introduction of furniture to his collection (pictured below), with multifunctional pieces designed to deal with the restrictions of smaller spaces. Creating both new furniture and tableware in addition to his existing range, Marc wants to offer a complete interior style.

Boase is currently known for his fresh approach to ceramics, so his move into furniture will be very interesting to watch. There is no doubt, however, that we can expect plenty more excitement from this modest, confident designer.

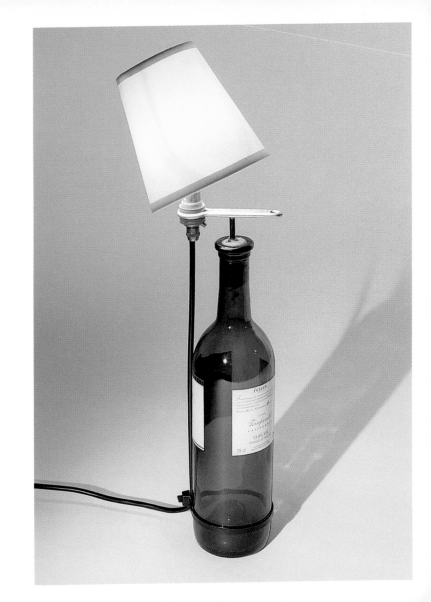

Carl Clerkin
Unit F1
2 – 4 Southgate Road
London N1 3JJ
020 7249 2021

AWARDS
Sainsbury's OXO Tower Scholarship (1998)
Kokuyo Design Award (1998)
Crafts Council Setting-Up Grant (1999)

DESIGN EVENTS
Salone Satellite, Milan Furniture Fair, Italy (April 1999)
100% Design, Earls Court, London (Sept 1999)
Young British Design, Cologne Furniture Fair, Germany (Jan 2000)
Alterpoint, Milan, Italy (April 2000)
Woody, Contemporary Applied Arts, London (Oct 2000)
About Time, Pure Living, London (Oct 2000)
Industry of One, Crafts Council, Islington, London (Feb–March 2001)

UK RETAILERS
Contact Carl Clerkin's studio for stockists

Born, bred and schooled in London, Carl Clerkin trained in furniture design at three of the city's best colleges – Central St Martin's, Middlesex University and the Royal College of Art. After graduating from the RCA in 1998, he moved into a Sainsbury Scholarship studio in the Oxo Tower, along with fellow graduate Gitta Gschwendtner (pp. 220–221).

Clerkin sees his two years at the RCA as an invaluable period of experimentation and a chance to come into contact with some of the world's finest creative minds. It was while at college that he began developing products for his 'Domestic Hardware' range, which he continues to work on today. Clerkin is not so much concerned with designing totally new objects, but instead turns his attention to recontextualizing everyday ephemera. One of the most remarkable 'Domestic Hardware' designs, for example, is a reworking of the bistro candle-in-a-wine-bottle. A celebration of the 'non-designed', this humorous piece, entitled 'Corkscrew Lamp' (pictured), uses the simplest components – a wine bottle, corkscrew, light fitting and shade – to create an object of disconcerting charm. Clerkin is clearly intrigued by the effect that mass-production has on our perceptions of what is designed and what is not, and how a simple product can – by a sleight of hand – be promoted to the level of desirable object.

The humble, transparent construction of his designs is simultaneously a paean to the everyday and a debunking of the design myth.

Clerkin's 'Bucket Seat' (pictured) is another witty piece in the 'Domestic Hardware' range. An industrial cleaning bucket is often turned upside down and used as a stool in times of need. Recognizing this and playing on its familiarity, Clerkin has replaced the basic bucket with a simple stool, retaining the handle as a sign of this domestic metamorphosis. The redefinition of the ready-made continues in other products in the range such as the 'Pie and Mash Tray', a cast-iron ashtray modelled on the form of a traditional pie-and-mash dish; 'S, M, L, XL', a selection of four picture frames that are hung from a clothes hanger with a tag indicating the 'garment' size.

Fascinated by 'people's incidental use of objects' and delighting in uncovering everyday serendipities, Clerkin is designer as conceptual artist. Despite the overt and rather harsh aesthetics of his products, the charm and humour of individual pieces seem likely to ensure his continuing success.

AMY CUSHING.MOSQUITO

Amy Cushing
62 Lower Ham Road
Kingston upon Thames
Surrey KT2 5AW
020 8715 5611
amycushing@mosquitodesign.com

Amy Cushing is one of Britain's best glass designers, creating vibrantly coloured and intricately formed glass tiles, platters and dishes that have set the standard in her field. She puts her present success down to the fact that, as a student at Chelsea College of Art and Design, she spent so much of her time experimenting with technique. So many of her contemporaries, Cushing thinks, were forced by the college system to specialize very early on in their apprenticeship, giving them very little time to make their own discoveries or to learn from their mistakes. Glass is an exceptionally difficult material with which to work, making an in-depth knowledge of technique crucial to good design. Cushing's trial-and-error approach at college, together with her rigorous recording of the results, was, she believes, the best possible way she could have learnt.

In 1997 Cushing set up Mosquito, the company name under which she trades today. Her range of glassware is all made by hand in her Wimbledon studio, with each meticulously produced piece the result of fresh thinking about pattern, proportion and colour. It was the last aspect of Cushing's work that first drew the attention of Paul Franzosi, owner of Set Pieces, who helped her to set up a collaborative project with the world-renowned glass-makers of Murano – Mosquito–Murano. Within a year Mosquito–Murano had produced an impressive 30-piece collection (pictured). Inevitably, given their origins, the vases and tableware that make up the collection are a feast for the eyes, but what makes these pieces truly original is Cushing's attention to texture and pattern and the sheer tactile quality she gives her material. Her belief in superlative production values meant that she made many trips to Venice in order to oversee the collection's manufacture.

The collection's complexity and diversity is awe-inspiring, and Cushing is justifiably proud of the outcome. Working with the renowned glass-makers in Murano was, she says, a massive privilege, and it clearly brought out the very best in her work. Cushing's achievement sends a clear message to UK manufacturers – success comes from one person's passion and another person's faith.

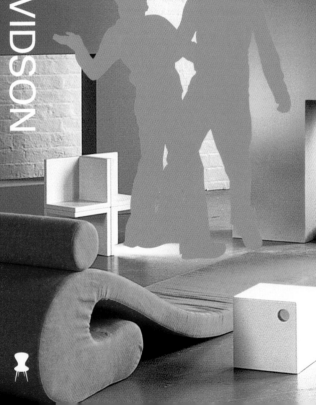

FIONA DAVIDSON

Fiona Davidson
Grand Duchess
Red Hill Lock
Ratcliffe-on-Soar
Nottingham NG11 0EB
01509 670 993
07967 183 453
fiona@grandduchess.freeserve.co.uk

AWARDS
100% Design/Crafts
Council Bursary
(Sept 1999)
East Midlands Arts and
Crafts Design Bursary
(Jan 2001)

DESIGN EVENTS
100% Design,
Earls Court, London
(Sept 1999)
Design Resolutions,
Royal Festival Hall,
London (Nov 1999)
Slab – The Form with No
Name, Mission, London
(Nov 1999–Jan 2000)
Creative Britain,
Berlin, Germany
(Jan–March 2000)
Big Torino 2000,
Turin Biennale, Turin,
Italy (April 2000)
East Up, Pure Living,
London (May–July 2000)
100% Design, with
Corian DuPont, Earls
Court, London (Oct 2000)
About Time, Pure Living,
London (Oct 2000)

UK RETAILERS
Pure Living, London
Contact Fiona Davidson's
studio for stockists

Fiona Davidson graduated in 1998, having taken a degree as a mature student in 3-D design at Loughborough College of Art and Design. She would never have predicted then that her final-year piece, 'Room Project 1', would attract so much attention, with the design press mesmerized by its extremely innovatory quality as well as by the thought-provoking issues that it unearths.

Davidson is a true visionary – a designer who is already looking ahead to the everyday problems that we are likely to confront in future years. By nature she is a problem-solver, working on solutions at a conceptual level well in advance of their actual implementation. 'Room Project 1' is a multifunctional furniture system that is designed to be totally adaptable to its user's needs and desires. Usually we never question the function of furniture – a chair is a chair is a chair. Davidson, however, wants 'to provoke a closer relationship between person, object and environment, challenging the notion of uncompromising and dictatorial products and questioning our perception of function'. The 'Room Project 1' comprises six interlocking yet separate forms, each of which lacks any single recognizable application and which therefore invite the user to use his or her imagination to construct a function,

almost as a child plays with building blocks. Davidson's aim is to encourage adult spatial awareness, as the active manipulation of the piece can considerably alter the surrounding environment in which it is placed. She is currently working on 'Room Project 2', which will be more commercially viable.

'Snail' (pictured) is another piece that is fully adaptable, a quality in this case achieved by using foam. The seating can be configured 'to provide comfort to suit the whims of the user', thereby challenging our definition of the word 'sitting'. In reality, the human being at rest sits, slouches, kneels, crouches, lounges, lies, stretches and curls – a fluid, self-determined, multipositionality that 'Snail' recognizes and seeks to nurture. A third piece, the 'Half Cube', is exactly that – a prototype that is like a simple three-sided corner section of a box. Following Davidson's lead, I will leave the reader to decide its various potential functions.

Fiona Davidson is a thought-provoking designer who is well ahead of her time. To ignore her work would be to deny yourself the vision of life as it could be.

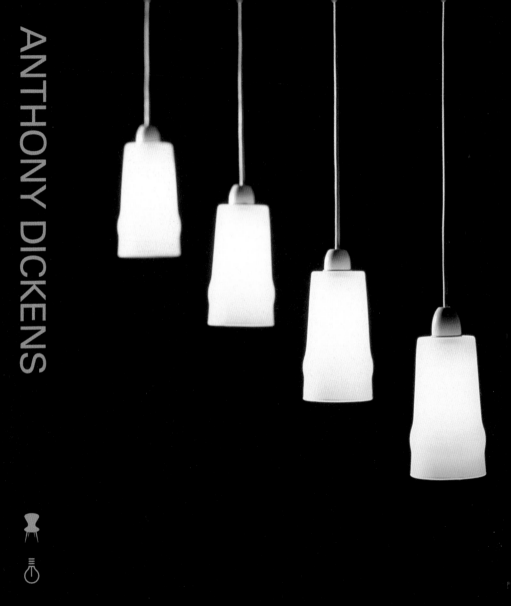

ANTHONY DICKENS

AWARDS
Purves & Purves Award for Product Design, New Designers (1997)
Contribution to Best Stand Design Award, New Designers (1997)

DESIGN EVENTS
Dub, Alterpoint, Milan, Italy (April 1999)
100% Design, Earls Court, London (Sept 1999)
Alterpoint, Milan, Italy (April 2000)
Illuminating British Lighting Design, NEC, Birmingham (Feb 2001)

UK RETAILERS
Purves & Purves
Contact Anthony Dickens' studio for other stockists

Anthony Dickens
Unit 8a
20 – 30 Wild's Rents
London SE1 4QG
020 7378 9399
07976 291 748
www.anthonydickens.com
ant@anthonydickens.com

A graduate of the Buckinghamshire Chilterns University course in Furniture and Related Product Design, Anthony Dickens' talent as a designer of innovative, quirky yet elegant lighting was quickly recognized when his 'Senecio' light won the 1997 Purves & Purves Award for Product Design. He confesses, however, that it is only relatively recently that he has begun to feel really happy about his work – a new-found confidence that has been undoubtedly bolstered by his impressive and diverse commissioning portfolio, which includes big names such as Andersen Consulting and Inflate, as well as by his appointment as an associate of JAM Communications.

In addition to the commissioned designs for bars, restaurants and cafés, such as the K-Bar and the Café des Artistes, Dickens has his own impressive product collection. His fresh, witty approach is seen at its simplest in his 'Happy Hour' pendant light, which features an upturned, sandblasted pint glass (pictured). A more recent creation is the 'Drip' light (pictured), which imitates the bulbous shape of a drip of water. All of Dickens' lights are simple and striking enough to make their mark either singly

or collectively as part of an installation, making them attractive for both domestic and contract use. Underlying such pieces' beautifully delicate, organic forms, though, are subtleties and twists that considerably deepen their appeal.

Dickens' ambitious, go-getting attitude is complemented by a modest, down-to-earth outlook that is always evident in his work. Having made a name for himself as an up-and-coming lighting designer, he has recently begun to turn to furniture design – evidence of a healthy desire for self-reinvention that will help make sure that his already blossoming design career will continue to grow.

ELLA DORAN

**Ella Doran
Unit H, Ground Floor South
95 – 97 Redchurch Street
London E2 7DJ
020 7729 8378
www.elladoran.co.uk
info@ella-doran.demon.co.uk**

Since setting up her own business, Ella Doran has rapidly established a secure place for herself in the design-oriented retail and gift markets. She first made her mark at the Earls Court Top Drawer gift show in 1996, attracting substantial coverage from the press as well as huge interest from retailers, despite the fact that at this stage her product range was quite limited.

Since then her selection has grown steadily. Simple natural forms, such as stones, water, leaves, fruit, vegetables, fish and flowers, adorn a wide range of pieces, including coasters, table mats, trays, crockery, mouse mats, roller blinds and wallpaper – with the imagery first recorded as photographs before being transferred to the designs. Doran is particularly alert to the textures and colours of the natural world, and her work is intended to alert the onlooker to the beauty and elegance of universally available but largely overlooked objects. She is currently working on an entirely new porcelain range.

Ella's enthusiasm, like her products, is inspiring. She tackles her business wholeheartedly and clearly hasn't allowed her rapid success go to her head. Not wanting her creativity to be sapped by paperwork, Ella has employed two assistants to deal with the burgeoning number of orders that flood in from across the globe.

Although busy, Ella still manages to find time for exhibitions, producing both limited editions and one-offs. She also collaborates with other designers such as Michael Marriott, and this helps her to push her creativity to the limits as well as creating a different focus from the commercial aspects that must always be considered when embarking upon larger production runs. No matter where she ventures from now on, Ella Doran will most certainly follow her heart every step of the way and will continue to make products that make people look and wonder.

CATERINA FADDA

AWARDS
Sainsbury's OXO Tower
Scholarship (1998)
100% Design/Crafts
Council Bursary (1999)
Peugeot Design Awards,
Lighting (1999)

DESIGN EVENTS
Salone Satellite,
Milan Furniture Fair,
Italy (April 1999)
Create British, Taipei
(March 1999)
100% Design, Earls Court,
London (Sept 1999)
Quality Britain, Manila,
Philippines (March 2000)
100% Design, Earls Court,
London (Oct 2000)
International Furniture
Fair Tokyo, Japan
(Nov 2000)
Switched On, Crafts
Council, Islington,
London (April–July 2001)

UK RETAILERS
Aero, London
Harrods, London
The Home, Bradford
Space, London
Vessel, London
Contact Caterina Fadda's
studio for other stockists

Caterina Fadda
Unit 1.08 Oxo Tower Wharf
Barge House Street
London SE1 9PH
020 7928 0024
www.caterinafadda.com
info@caterinafadda.com

Caterina Fadda graduated from the Royal College of Art in ceramics and glass in 1997 and, as a recipient of the Sainsbury's Scholarship, was able to establish herself quickly in her Oxo Tower shop and studio space. The strength of her college work and its advanced level of development meant she was in a position to start manufacturing her plates and bowls almost immediately. At its launch, her 'Cellule' collection of ceramic dinner plates won attention due to its fluid, amoebic forms and interactive multifunctionality. Her innovative approach to form and function can also be seen in her 'Kiko' ceramic serving bowls (pictured), with their sweeping, graceful lines and pure organic forms.

Like all good designers, Fadda is constantly looking to add something new and fresh to her work. Her determination to remain at the creative forefront is most evident in her award-winning 'Sasso' light. Inside its chunky, pebble-like, free-blown glass form is a layer of colour – either red or white – that masks the bulb and creates a warm, relaxing glow when the unit is illuminated. The piece is technologically innovative, too. Power is supplied to the lamp via a strip of electrical steel tape that runs along its clear acrylic base, so that placing the lamp onto the strip or removing it turns the unit on or off.

Other products by Fadda include 'A Maze', a modular acrylic table, and 'SAL&', pillow-like ceramic salt and pepper shakers that are now manufactured by Authentics. A more recent addition is a cylindrical acrylic fruit bowl that is criss-crossed with woven nylon thread. The nylon acts as an aerating base for the fruit, keeping it fresh for longer.

Fadda's versatility with a variety of materials is a crucial key to both her creative development and her appeal in what is a hugely competitive industry. She anticipates a move into plastics, rubber or leather and will no doubt subject these materials to the same transformative vision she has realized elsewhere. If Caterina Fadda maintains her innovative design approach, she is sure to excel even her own expectations.

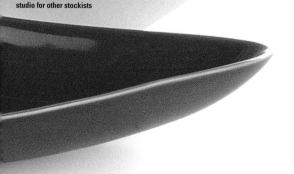

FIREWORKS

Fireworks
35A Dalhousie Street
Glasgow G3 6PW
0141 332 4969
tomelliott@fireworksceramics.co.uk

Tom Elliott graduated in ceramics from the Glasgow School of Art in 1993 and, with partner Jacki Alexander, set up Fireworks Ceramic Workshop in 1996, in a location close to his former college. Initially the duo concentrated on producing handmade one-offs with a very craft-led approach, and it wasn't until relatively recently that they started working with industry. Fireworks' range of tableware has made an important contribution to ceramics' current upsurge in popularity and its full acceptance as a 'contemporary' discipline.

Elliott believes that 'the best domestic products make everyday tasks more enjoyable', and it is this simple philosophy that he aims to carry through his designs. The 'Porcini' range (pictured) is a perfect illustration of his goals, with multifunctionality combining with appealing design and a sense of fun. The espresso cup and saucer, for example, can be turned upside down and used as an egg cup and egg warmer; the cappuccino cup and saucer could be used as a dip bowl; while the larger vessels work beautifully as multi-course receptacles – for a soup and then a pasta or rice dish, for example. This commendable range was shortlisted for the Peugeot Design Awards in 1999 and is now available internationally. Another piece that raises eyebrows and puts smiles on faces is the intriguing 'Crumpled Vase', whose design derives from the familar sight of a crumpled piece of paper or fabric and relies on superlative manipulation of its material for its realization. The joke and beauty, of course, lie in the *trompe-l'oeil* that briefly prevails before the viewer discovers that the vase is in fact made of ceramic.

Like all true creatives, Elliott is constantly looking for new challenges and directions. However, even I was quite surprised to hear that he is envisaging a revival of chintz. Sick of what he calls the 'good taste' aesthetic that is 'devoid of any kind of integrity or thought', Elliott wants to produce work in a variety of materials that will playfully and wilfully offend our sense of what consitutes good design. If the thought of something like 'New Century Chintz' fills you with horror, you're not alone, but in view of the designer's past achievements and the refined elegance of which he has already proven himself capable, perhaps we should just wait and see.

Gitta Gschwendtner
Unit F1
2 – 4 Southgate Road
London N1 3JJ
020 7249 2021

In the three years that have passed since she graduated from the Royal College of Art, the German-born furniture designer Gitta Gschwendtner has made some impressive achievements, working on her own designs as well as product development for a variety of large design companies, including Horm, Lloyd Loom and Habitat (see pp. 88 – 89). Her training has been thorough. After studying at two top institutions, Central St Martin's College of Art and Design and Kingston University, she embarked on what she calls 'two years of self-indulgence' at the prestigious Royal College of Arts. Gschwendtner's time at the college proved to be both extremely productive and inspirational. Alongside fellow student Angel Monzón, she won a competition to design and refurbish the Beck's Artbar at

the RCA, which gave her additional confidence as well as first-hand experience of the world she was about to enter.

A crucial and challenging part of becoming a designer is getting yourself noticed, but fortunately Gschwendtner had overcome this hurdle even before graduating. In May 1998, with fellow student Carl Clerkin (see pp. 206–207), she won one of ten Sainsbury's scholarships

AWARDS
Sainsbury's OXO Tower
scholarship (1998)
Kokuyo Design Award
(1998)
Crafts Council
'Setting-Up Grant (1998)

DESIGN EVENTS
Salone Satellite, Milan
Furniture Fair, Italy
(April 1999)
100% Design, Earls Court,
London (Sept 1999)
Design Resolutions,
Royal Festival Hall,
London (Nov 1999)
Young British Design,
Cologne Furniture Fair,
Germany (Jan 2000)
Alterpoint, Milan Furniture
Fair, Italy (April 2000)
100% Design, with Corian
DuPont, Earls Court,
London (Oct 2000)
Industry of One, Crafts
Council, London
(Feb–March 2001)

UK RETAILERS
Pure Living, London
Contact studio for stockists

for a one-year tenancy of studio space in London's Oxo Tower. Her degree show in July 1998 also proved a success, with two large international production companies snapping up her 'Strangled Light' (pictured) and 'Sliding Box' shelving.

It is Gschwendtner's unique ability to combine formal simplicity with an element of surprise and humour that captures attention. 'My works deals with preconceptions about objects,' the designer says, 'engaging the user to explore what is normally taken for granted.' 'Strangled Light', for example, challenges our preconceptions of what constitutes a pendant light, normally made up of a standard light fitting and cable, plus a detachable lampshade. Gitta's light, however, transforms the usual functional role of the cable into an integral part of the design, where it takes the form of a noose that quite literally strangles the ceramic shade and seems to determine its shape. It is this kind of humour that makes Gitta's work so refreshing, provoking an interaction, between viewer and piece.

Her 'Magazine Rug' (pictured) is a similarly simple yet effective product. The rippling folds of a kicked rug are a commonplace irritation. Gschwendtner gives a structure to the folds and makes them into a holder for magazines and books. The user can thus enjoy the comfort of sitting on the goat-skin rug while flicking through the pages of a book. Here, as the designer says, 'Luxury and leisure are paired with humour and surprise, while functionality is maintained.'

Gschwendtner has designed many other similarly playful and challenging products, including tables, chairs, fruit bowls and lights. Because she is not restricted to one style, material, or product type, her collection has an unpredictable diversity. It is important for Gschwendtner to push and question disciplinary boundaries in order to keep her creative energy alive and it is obvious that there is plenty more to come from this talented and experimental designer.

AWARDS
Glasgow Collection Award for Design and Innovation (1999)
Glasgow Design Enterprise Award (Dec 1999)

DESIGN EVENTS
The Glasgow Collection, The Lighthouse, Glasgow (1999)
100% Design, Earls Court, London (Sept 1999)
The Glasgow Collection, The Lighthouse, Glasgow (Jan 2000)
Art for Europe, Brussels, Belgium (Dec 2000-Dec 2001)

UK RETAILERS
The National Trust for Scotland, Glasgow
Places & Spaces, London
Pure Living, London
Contact Happell's studio for other stockists

Happell
256 High Street
Glasgow G4 0QT
0141 400 2600
www.happell.co.uk
info@happell.co.uk

Dene Happell graduated in sculpture from the Glasgow School of Art in 1994. His route to becoming a designer has been an indirect evolution. Even at college, his sculpture possessed a clean, rather designed look, so it hardly came as a surprise when he began to play with 'functional sculpture', developing some of his ideas into pieces of furniture.

Happell won his first design project when entrepreneur Colin MacDougal commissioned him to carry out the interior design of the bar/restaurant Air Organic in Glasgow (pictured). Dene rose to the challenge and triumphed. Air Organic opened in August 1998 and instantly became a big hit. Other projects followed, including the refurbishment of Rab Ha's hotel and restaurant in Glasgow's Merchant City; furniture and lighting for the reception and bar areas in Groucho Saint Judes; and the design of the café/bar Four in Glasgow's Centre for Contemporary Arts.

Happell launched his own product range at 100% Design in 1999. His 'Low' table (pictured) attracted international attention and was awarded the prestigious Glasgow Collection Award for design and innovation. Meeting an increasing demand for multifunctionality, the table

can revolve 360°, giving easy access to the various storage compartments built into its body. Happell also designed a ceramic ashtray, bowl and vase that can all fit into the table top, allowing the user to adapt the feel and function of the table. The table can be specified in more than a hundred colours and finishes, making it adaptable to any setting.

Happell's 'Wallglow' and 'Boxglow' lights both utilize a single sheet of ash veneer. When switched off, the lights give the impression of being solid blocks of wood. As soon as they are illuminated, however, a warm, textured light glows through the veneer.

A recent interior project – Its Organic – a new soup and juice bar franchise in Edinburgh's West End, included the design of a new table called 'Snoop', which functions not only as a table but also as a chair and storage unit. Dene's vision is clear: to continue producing 'fresh and innovative designs, while always working with a twist that remains unique, warm and friendly'.

HIVE

Hive
Unit 1.02 Oxo Tower Wharf
Barge House Street
London SE1 9PH
020 7261 9791
www.hivespace.com
hive@hivespace.com

Hive's partners Monika Piatkowski and Mark Dyson met while studying at Glasgow School of Art nearly ten years ago. They began working together on various collaborative projects after they graduated. Piatkowski's training as a graphic designer took her into televisual graphics and corporate identity, while Dyson's architectural training led him to several renowned practices. The marriage of Piatkowski's 'visual clarity' and Dyson's 'functional rationality' has proved incredibly successful.

Working with felt when others were excited by plastics, the duo was in a strong position to be noticed. When the 1998 Sainsbury scholarship scheme to win one of ten studios in the Oxo Tower was announced, Piatkowski entered with the 'Pail' felt bucket. She won a place and Hive was officially born on London's South Bank.

The excitement and interest generated by journalists was hugely encouraging. Pioneers of felt (the material) received new acclaim and consequently Hive's 'Pail' vessel, 'Boxer' bags (pictured), and 'Handbag' books attracted the attention of international buyers. Not wanting to be known solely for their use of felt,

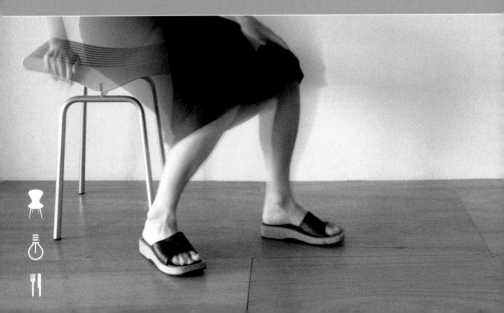

Hive followed this success by developing a small range of furniture. Launched at 100% Design in 1999, the prototypes were well received.

When designing, Hive is interested in reinventing the invented: taking an identifiable object and 'subjecting it to a re-examination', giving it fresh, ironic and rather playful new values. Clearly influenced by Duchamp, the 'Trike' magazine rack, for example, takes the bicycle frame as its structural mainpiece and throws it into a new context, remaining subtle and yet painfully clear.

'Different stories come through in the products with the inclusion of the ready-made sneaking it's way into something that looks very clean.' The beauty of Hive's work is the seemingly effortless combination of this 'knowing irony' with a style that remains visually clean and pleasing to the eye.

The future sees Hive becoming an increasingly multi-disciplinary studio, continuing to produce its own ranges but also working on commissions for interior projects. With their combined experience of product, interior, graphic and architectural design, Piatkowski and Dyson feel they can bring a clarity and consistency to commissions that others may lack, and have a lot to offer clients.

With a range of leather accessories launched at 100% Design in 2000, it's obvious that these enthusiastic designers will continue to explore new directions, constantly challenging function, materials and themselves.

HUB

Hub
Suite 12, Level 4
New England House
New England Street
Brighton BN1 4GH
01273 385 684
www.hub-design.co.uk

Enthusiastic duo Andrew Tanner and Anna Thomson formed Hub in 1998, having both graduated from the University of Brighton in 3-D design. Andrew's sculptural turn of mind and Anna's astute knowledge of production was deemed to be a successful creative partnership and led to the development of an excellent range of ceramic lighting, tiles and tableware.

With financial support from the Prince's Trust, Hub was able to launch commercially at the Top Drawer exhibition in August 1999, attracting considerable attention for its contemporary twist on a traditional material. Hub's objective is to 'blur the boundaries between sculpture and function', while at the same time avoiding dictating to the consumer the exact function its products should perform. 'Crate', for example, acts perfectly as a fruit bowl, but Hub's desire to 'design the ultimate blank canvas for food' has even seen one restaurant use the 'Crate' as a platter on which to serve oysters.

All of their products evolve from forms and concepts that have been inspired by a wide diversity of sources, including art, the environment and even biological structures. Hub are interested in introducing colour to what is currently a predominantly white product range, working with fashion and trend predictors on 'the future hues'. Two new tableware ranges, 'Lap' (pictured) and 'Tag', were launched at Top Drawer in the summer of 2000. For innovative lighting, tiles and tableware, keep a close eye on these fresh faces.

TOM KIRK

AWARDS
100% Design/ Crafts
Council Bursary (1998)
Ergonom Product
Development Award
(1999)

DESIGN EVENTS
Create Britain, Taipei
(March 1999)
Salone del Mobile,
Milan Furniture Fair,
Italy (April 1999)
Mode, Business Design
Centre, Islington,
London (June 1999)
100% Design,
Earls Court, London
(Sept 1999)
Design Resolutions,
Royal Festival Hall,
London (Nov 1999)
Exposition de Design
Britannique, Silvera,
Paris, France (Jan 2000)
New York Gift Fair,
USA (Jan 2000, 2001)
Contemporary Decorative
Arts, Sotheby's, London
(Feb 2000, 2001)
International Furniture
Fair, New York, USA
(May 2000)
Industry of One, Crafts
Council, Islington, London
(Feb–March 2001)

UK RETAILERS
Ferrious, Manchester
Noel Hennessy Furniture,
London
Mint, London
Places & Spaces, London
Space, London
Whippet, London
Contact Tom Kirk's
studio for stockists

Tom Kirk
13c Camberwell Church Street
London SE5 8TR
020 7780 9288
tomkirk@excite.co.uk

Tom Kirk graduated from Camberwell College of Art in silversmithing and metalwork in 1994. Even as a student, though, Kirk's interests already leant towards lighting design. For a few years, he worked as a sales consultant in the lighting department at Heal's (see pp. 92–93) and at the London Lighting Company (see pp. 122–23), while carrying out commissions in a tiny shared studio unit on his days off. In January 1997 he gave up his job and committed himself fully to his design work, presenting his first collection in the 'New Designers' section at 100% Design in September 1997. The press attention was favourable and introduced his name and style to a wider design world.

Kirk is ostensibly concerned with the effect of light when used in conjunction with interesting materials and forms rather than in the light source itself. Diffusing, masking, shrouding and borrowing light, he aims to achieve visually exciting objects through contrasts in texture, material and colour. So far one of Kirk's most successful pieces has been the 'Spike' wall light (detail pictured) – an anodized aluminium box housing a light source that when switched on illuminates spike-like polyester-resin elements set into the box surface. The elements are available in any colour and are all laboriously handmade in Kirk's workshop. While the piece's clean, regimented construction implies mass-production, the varied, inconsistent appearance of the swirling resin spikes creates a unique tension.

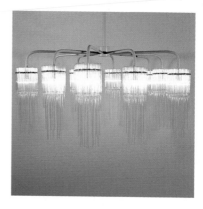

His exciting 'GS' series of chandeliers (pictured), pendant and wall lights are fairly new additions to his range. While experimenting with industrially produced tapered glass straws, Kirk hit on the idea of using them as repeated components in an innovative alternative to more traditional forms of lamps and chandeliers. Hanging rather tentatively like icicles from a metal plate, the straws collectively distort the light source and take on a glowing, sparkling appearance – the effect is mesmerizing. Other lights in his range include the elegant sandblasted borosilicate-glass 'CS' floor and table lights and the 'Turf' table light, which uses frosted soda-lime glass rods.

Kirk enjoys working to commission and will happily create unique lighting solutions to meet any requirements. With recent commissions from MTV Europe, the Breakfast Group, Donna Karan, the End Nightclub, the Annexe Bar and Ozer Restaurant, Kirk's unique aesthetic is obviously catching on.

AWARDS
100% Design/Crafts
Council Bursary (1998)
Scandinavian Award,
Business Link (Oct 2000)
Designer Europeo award,
Italy (2000)

DESIGN EVENTS
Salone Satellite, Milan
Furniture Fair, Italy
(April 1999)
100% Design,
Earls Court, London
(Sept 1999)
Chelsea Crafts Fair,
London (1999)
International Furniture
Fair Tokyo, Japan
(Nov 2000)
Chelsea Crafts Fair,
London (2000)

UK RETAILERS
The Conran Shop, London
Caterina Fadda Studio,
London
Contact the Maké Design
studio for stockists

Maké Design
Block A, Unit 8
1 Fawe Street
London E14 6PD
020 7515 0602
www.makedesign.co.uk
li@makedesignltd.demon.co.uk

Li Marbahan and Colin Smith set up Maké Design Ltd in London in 1994, producing elegantly understated domestic furniture and accessories. Marbahan, the design half of the team, took an interesting route into the world of design. Originally from Singapore and born to a Chinese mother and Javanese/Japanese father, he has been living in the UK for the last eighteen years. For two years he worked in hairdressing, until, driven by creative frustration, he enrolled on a 3-D design course at Polytechnic Southwest in Exeter. There he gained a powerful knowledge of materials and forms as well as the creative freedom that enabled him to establish his own style, fusing oriental concepts with Western technologies. After graduation, he undertook traditional woodworking and kitchen-making before eventually deciding to work on his own pieces. It was at this stage that he met Colin Smith, whose knowledge of finance, marketing and promotion have proved invaluable in the realization of Marbahan's creative vision.

Marbahan's distinctive designs combine minimal production wastage with maximum material manipulation. Working with Aero-ply – a material formed from ultra-thin layers of birch plywood – the designer exploits the wood's flexibility through curving, bending and folding, almost origami-style. Working with layers of birch plywood ranging from 0.4 to 1.2 millimetres in thickness, Marbahan carefully constructs each piece by hand in his East End workshop. Deeply concerned by society's excessive and inefficient use of resources, Marbahan ensures that each piece does not exceed wastage of more than 5 to 10 per cent.

All of Marbahan's pieces have been carefully scrutinized using Computer Aided Design (CAD), providing solutions to problems without the need for much physical modelling and thereby helping to keep wastage and prototyping costs down. The result is a collection that combines minimalist beauty, functional practicality, and, ultimately, commercial viability. Because Marbahan's skilled method of production is difficult to accommodate on a large scale, the pieces don't command mass-production affordability, although Marbahan and Smith point out that their durability and quality more than justify their cost.

Marbahan believes that all products should be a near-permanent enhancement of their environment and that, if this were to be achieved, our 'disposable culture' would disappear. It is for this reason that Maké Design's stackable table (pictured), tray, magazine rack, shelf, mirror and CD rack are unobtrusive and understated and so unlikely to date. Maké Design's concern for the environment has been recognized by the Department of Trade and Industry as a model for design excellence, and their pieces have been used by the government to promote British industry and innovation. However, it seems that Marbahan won't be fully satisfied until he has designed something that is entirely waste-free!

GERALDINE MCGLOIN

Geraldine McGloin
Unit 232
Stratford Workshops
Burford Road
London E15 2SP
020 8503 1030
www.geraldinemcgloin.com
geraldine@geraldinemcgloin.com

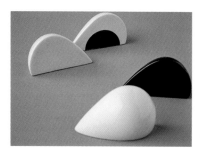

Geraldine McGloin's path to becoming an independent ceramicist has been a rather long and convoluted one. After leaving school in 1983, she dabbled in decorating, silk-screen printing, model-making and prototyping before finally embarking on a degree course in ceramics at London's University of Westminster. Geraldine rebelled against the traditional image of ceramics presented on the course, designing work that was geared towards commercial production rather than to one-off pieces. After graduating, she worked for C.P. Ceramics, a company that undertakes model-making, mould-making, slip-casting and prototyping for clients such as Eurolounge, Habitat, Babylon Design and Worldwide Co. Having gained an insight into the production process, McGloin began to design her own range of tableware and giftware with factory manufacturing in mind. In April 1999 she took the plunge and set up her own studio in the East End, where she today designs and produces slip-cast semi-porcelain, porcelain and china tableware. Exhibiting on a shared stand with Fiona Davidson (see pp. 210–211) at 100% Design in 1999 forced Geraldine to produce a variety of designs, which she continues to expand today.

Despite her interest in mass-produced ceramics, the Irish-born designer stresses the importance of quality craftsmanship.

She can't bear to see a beautiful porcelain vase that, when turned upside down, reveals a rather shabby and neglected underside. For McGloin this exposes a product of surface beauty only, lacking any real sincerity or integrity. McGloin's ultimate ambition is to reconcile the cost-effectiveness and efficiency of manufacture with the high quality achievable by hand-crafted techniques. Since she recognizes that her ideal is near unrealizable under modern market conditions, she has resorted, albeit reluctantly, to the hands-on approach.

McGloin's vases, beakers, dishes and cups are certainly meticulously produced. Her increasingly multifunctional selection of tableware, such as the 'Bean' range (pictured) of snaking, segmented dishes, is not lavishly decorated but is restricted to black or white finishes. She sometimes adds simple geometric transfers, which gives them an additional individual twist. All of the designer-maker's pieces are made in her studio, so it's possible to speak to her personally and order the exact configurations and colours you want.

NELSON

Nelson
PO Box 17357
London SW9 0WB
020 8519 8694
www.members.aol.com/nelsonpage
jfnelson1@aol.com

Since its introduction in 1879, numerous designers have tried to deal with the problem of how to house the humble filament bulb. Lighting design pioneers, such as Poul Henningsen, Achille Castiglioni, Vico Magistretti, Richard Sapper and Ingo Maurer, have all taken lighting to new levels in their time, and today's designers – including Tom Dixon, Jasper Morrison, Babylon Design, and Proto Design – have produced their own forward-thinking innovations. Positioned independently from this mainstream, however, is Julie Nelson.

After graduating from Middlesex University in 3-D design, Nelson worked for many years as a sculptor and model-maker in television, theatre and advertising and developed a 'distinctive feel for form and the importance of light on a 3-D shape'. It was her experimentation with fluid forms that led her to working with light. Inspired by Scandinavian organic modernism, Julie worked on a range of ceramic lights, launched at the first-ever 100% Design exhibition in 1995. In 1997 she established her own company, Nelson.

The beauty of Julie Nelson's lights is their unique dual function. At night-time they emit a lovely ambient light, while in the day they stand alone as works of sculpture. This alluring multifunctionality is heightened by the designer's use of ceramic, a material not traditionally associated with lighting. Nelson, however, loves its opacity and the 'way the light bounces around and fills recesses, accentuating the form'.

Nelson currently has fifteen lights in her collection, which sells internationally. The most recent additions to the range are the 'Porous' table and wall lights, which were first exhibited in the Salone Satellite at the Milan Furniture Fair in April 2000. These are made from metal and wood, but Nelson is becoming increasingly interested in working with other materials, too. Moreover, there is an indication of a move into furniture with the 'Crater' fibreglass seat (pictured below), presently at prototype stage. It's encouraging to see Julie Nelson's enthusiasm carrying her into new territory.

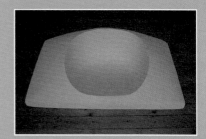

**One Foot Taller
203–205 Firhill Road
Glasgow G20 7SD
0141 946 8666**

One Foot Taller was established in 1995 by Katarina Barac and the 'one-foot-taller' Will White soon after graduating together from the Glasgow School of Art in product design. Their multidisciplinary studio was originally intended as a design consultancy, but they soon realized that producing their own product line was their only way to get noticed in a fiercely competitive design world. The decision meant hands-on manufacturing and marketing, building up a name and reputation through international trade fairs. While selling their affordable range of bowls and accessories, they were also beginning work on a few local consultancy projects.

In 1997 the duo was approached by Habitat (see pp. 88–89) to design two ranges of kitchen storage, and they went on to design and prototype a table and chairs for textile designers Timorous Beasties. In 1998 One Foot Taller moved into the international spotlight with the production of the 'Chasm' chair for Nice House in Glasgow. This unique piece is manufactured by the process of rotation moulding, which is cheaper than the more sophisticated injection moulding. The strange, two-legged bulbous form that appears from the mould is cut in half down the middle and the two sections swapped around and simply bolted together. The chair exposes its hollow core, making the inside a feature in its own right. The success of the chair led to several awards including Overall Winners of the Peugeot Design Awards in 1999.

Since then, One Foot Taller has developed the 'Canyon' and 'Ravine' armchairs, bigger and beefier cousins to the 'Chasm'. Another exciting initiative has been a collaborative project with Timorous Beasties, designing the interior of restaurant/bar Strata on Glasgow's Queen Street (above), which included the impressive installation of a bone-china lamp designed in collaboration with Fireworks (see pp. 218–19) and supported by the prestigious Glasgow Collection.

In the future the company aims to continue working on consultancy projects, while continuing to develop their own product range. Having had a taster of mass production, they would like to pursue opportunities in this direction and are currently interested in the intervention of electrical components into their work. This is just one of many thoughts that are kicking around in the highly imaginative minds that make up this forward-thinking design partnership.

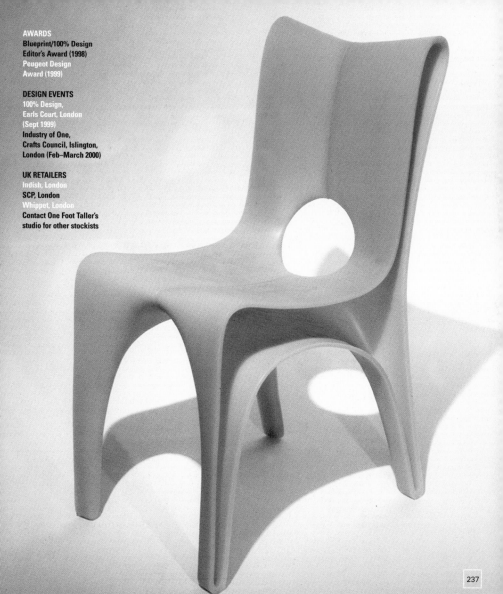

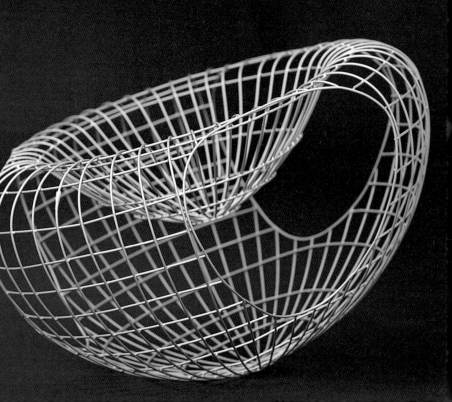

MAX SHEPHERD

Max Shepherd
Unit 2E
35 – 40 Charlotte Road
London EC2A 3DH
07989 555 354
www.maxshepherd.net
max@maxshepherd.net

AWARDS
New Designer of the Year Award, New Designers Exhibition (1997)

DESIGN EVENTS
Alterpoint, Milan
Furniture Fair, Italy
(April 1999)
Create Britain, Taipei
(March 1999)
100% Design,
Earls Court, London
(Sept 1999)

UK RETAILERS
Contact Max Shepherd's studio for stockists

A 1997 graduate in 3-D design from Leeds Metropolitan University, Max Shepherd has worked on an impressive array of projects, in particular contributing designs to the UK's growing bar scene. He began by working on tables for the interior of the Sac Bar on Soho's Greek Street and then moved on to assist designer Ou Baholyodhin (see pp. 84 – 85) on designs for the nearby K-Bar on Wardour Street. Three more K-Bars followed, and with each one his responsibility grew. After working alongside Baholyodhin on a variety of projects in Japan, Max took on his first solo job in April 1999, as project director for the South Circular Bar in Clapham, London. He is currently setting up his very own bar in Central London, where, he assures me, he intends to implement an exciting new concept in bar design.

Remarkably, Shepherd also finds time to design cutting-edge furniture and accessories. Like his products, he is multifaceted and likes to work on several projects at once, allowing his creativity to be continually tested by fresh challenges. Until recently Shepherd had only a few pieces to his name, such as the ethereal 'WhY?' armchair (pictured), which takes its humourous inspiration from a pair of men's underpants. A new range of products and accessories, however, aims at being more commercially viable and affordable.

Shepherd's sculptural designs are made 'to blur the boundaries of utility', preferring not to dictate their function to the user. The 'Round Box Storage' can be used for whatever your imagination dreams up, '...from bedside table and dirty-washing basket to a floor light or coffee table'. Shepherd likes to put contrasting values into a product, 'with one aspect being very serious and the other humorous'. Max's laid-back, live-for-the-moment attitude makes him hard to predict, but one thing's for certain, whatever he works on, he will continue to produce innovative and exciting results.

Bodo Sperlein
Unit 1.12 Oxo Tower Wharf
Barge House Street
London SE1 9PH
020 7633 9413
bodo@bodosperlein.com

A 1997 graduate from the 3-D design course at Camberwell College of Art, Bodo Sperlein has rapidly established himself as one of the UK's leading ceramacists. The initial impetus for his career, he says, came when he tried to buy tableware for his London flat. Disliking the designs of the pieces he could afford and the high prices of those he liked, he decided to come up with his own products, despite a tutor's warnings that there was no money to be made from ceramics. At a time when the whole of the design world seemed fixated on bright plastics and frosted glass, Sperlein determined to bring ceramics 'into the 21st century'.

Sperlein's first range attracted considerable attention at the New Designers exhibition in 1997, where its textural and tactile qualities set it apart. Such qualities – rather than colour – are primary ones for the designer, who believes that his distinctive forms are best brought out by the purity and translucency of bone china. The delicate, flowing forms he achieves from his material are astonishing and fulfil Sperlein's objective to move ceramics away from 'just teapots, cups and little flowerpots'.

The subtlety and purity of Sperlein's designs have won him an impressive number of commissions, including a range of ceramic wares for Browns Living on London's South Molton Street (see pp. 40 – 41) and an extensive lighting, table and giftware collection for Nymphenburg, one of Europe's oldest porcelain manufacturers. He is particularly keen to work in this way – adding fresh ideas to well-established companies and brand names. Although currently busy developing ceramics, metal, glass and stone products for various companies as well as producing a porcelain perfume bottle for a British fashion house, Sperlein certainly does not want to lose sight of his own range.

All of his work can be viewed at his Oxo Tower studio on London's South Bank, which also doubles up as a shop and showroom. As with all design objects, it's important to be able to touch the pieces before purchasing – a principle with which the designer certainly agrees.

Sponge
14 Victor Road
London NW10 5XE
020 8969 6609
www.spongedesigns.com

Otto Lauterbach came to London from his
home country of Venezuela in order to
make music. However, while working in
Notting Hill's The Sugar Club restaurant
(now Bali Sugar), he met the well-known
designer Tom Dixon of Eurolounge and
was invited to train in the Eurolounge
studio, where he stayed for a year.
Lauterbach had originally studied fine
art in Caracas, and at Eurolounge he was
exposed to the possibility of combining
the sculptural with functionality, thereby
challenging preconceptions about what
constitutes art and what functional design.

Lauterbach was selling one-off pieces
to Places and Spaces (see pp. 150 – 51) in
Clapham when he met Anthony Dickenson,
who swiftly spotted the potential in his
work. In the spring of 1998, when Anthony
introduced Otto to the owners of Licious
in Oxford, Lauterbach proposed setting up
Sponge.

The designer's fine-art training has
stuck with him to this day as he continues
to develop his creations in a very hands-on
manner. Lauterbach does not use a
computer at any stage of the design
process, preferring instead to get his hands
dirty in the workshop. Even if he were to
start using a computer one day, it's clear
that it would never replace the nitty-gritty
material processes that Lauterbach so
strongly believes in.

The designer experiments with
sculptural forms first and then brings
in the functional element second, thereby
creating pieces that can stand alone in a
space as artwork. He recounts an occasion

when, at a trade exhibition, Sponge had
one of its pieces, the 'OTS' CD rack,
standing empty on a plinth, and he was
overjoyed when people walked around it
and said, 'Wow! What is it?' The 'Heartbeat'
coat rail is similarly mysterious, and it is
this multifunctional openness that makes
Sponge's work so special. The slightly
more obvious 'Big Bean' rocking chair
(pictured) was a huge hit at the 1999 100%
Design show at Earls Court and made
it to the finals of the Blueprint/100%
Design Awards, attracting a lot of press
and retail attention.

Sponge is not only about products;
it has also moved into interiors, too, with
a design for a bar in London's fashionable
Shoreditch called the Pool, which
opened in November 1999. 'Such a great
experience', Lauterbach recalls, 'but so
many restrictions – it was a real eye-opener.'

Lauterbach's and Dickenson's
desire to avoid the trendy, elitist status
often associated with the design world
is certainly a breath of fresh air. They
consider themselves to be more artists
than designers and want to introduce new
artists into the company who will share
their same innovative vision.

EL ULTIMO GRITO

AWARDS
**Blueprint /100% Design
Award (1997, 1998, 1999)**
Peugeot Design
Award (1999)

DESIGN EVENTS
Salone Satellite, Milan
Furniture Fair, Italy
(April 1999)
**100% Design, Earls Court,
London (Sept 1999)**
Designers Block, Brick
Lane, London (Sept 1999)
**Design Resolutions,
Royal Festival Hall,
London (Nov 1999)**
Contemporary
Decorative Arts,
Sotheby's, London
(Feb 2000)
**Hidden, Milan Furniture
Fair, Italy (April 2000)**
100% Design, Earls Court,
London (Oct 2000)
**Industry of One,
Crafts Council,
Islington, London
(Feb– March 2001)**

UK RETAILERS
**Contact El Ultimo Grito's
studio for stockists**

**El Ultimo Grito
4 Peacock Yard
Iliffe Street
London SE17
020 7739 1009**

The Spanish furniture, lighting, product and interior design trio Roberto Feo, Rosario Hurtado and Francisco Santos formed London-based design company El Ultimo Grito ('The Last Shout') in 1997. As a group, El Ultimo Grito is uniquely open to experimentation, developing innovative reinventions of everyday objects that are both humorous and refreshing.

The design team aims to provide simple, quirky solutions to ordinary needs. At the heart of all their work is a careful observation of daily, domestic routines and a readiness to reinterpret existing materials and mechanisms. El Ultimo Grito's 'Miss Ramirez' easy chair (pictured), which won the Blueprint/100% Design Award in 1997, is a case in point. Formed from an unusual combination of cork and latex, the chair provides a unique and surprising seating experience, allowing the body to adapt comfortably to its ergonomic form. As the chair is also quite heavy, its design includes the provision of casters on the front legs to ease movement.

Since 1998 the trio has been working on a series of designs entitled 'Minimal Maximum', which combines minimal use of material with maximum expression. One of the first pieces in this collection was 'Mind the Gap', a coffee table with integrated magazine rack. A gap in the middle of the rubber table top forms a flexible storage space for magazines and newspapers. This simple, witty design won a Blueprint/100% Design Award in 1998 and the Peugeot Design Award for Furniture in 1999.

In 1999 El Ultimo Grito designed 'Good Morning Moneypenny', a coat rack constructed from a sheet of polypropylene and old magazines. The polypropylene sheet, into which a series of holes has first been cut, is rolled into a tube and old magazines or newspapers are then rolled up and inserted through the holes, forming baton-like hooks that are strong, recyclable and fun.

A recent addition to the El Ultimo Grito range is a spring-loaded laundry bin entitled 'What goes down ...must come up'. A bag made from orange 'kite' fabric is suspended from four tension rings within a simple stainless-steel frame. The springs give with the weight of added clothes and consequently the bag grows, touching the floor when it is full. As the bag is unloaded, the weight decreases and the springs pull the bag back to the top, meaning you don't have to scrabble around for that last solitary sock!

This attention to everyday practicality couples with sensible use of materials to give El Ultimo Grito's products their long-lasting character. European manufacturers are now beginning to snap up these products, and the trio is clearly destined for great things.

LYNNE WILSON

1st Floor Studio
14 Bacon Street
London E1 6LF
0207 613 1675
lynnewilson@exl.co.uk

Lynne Wilson graduated in furniture design from Edinburgh College of Art in 1996. While studying, Lynne recalls taking a somewhat non-commercial stance on her designs, enjoying the creative freedom that, fortunately, students are able to exercise. It is unusual then to find out that she produced the well-known 'Loopy' table (pictured) while still at college. There was considerable interest in the table at her degree show and the New Designers exhibition in 1996, so Wilson embarked on the long, rocky road to getting it manufactured.

With tables already in The Conran Shop and Purves & Purves before the production techniques had been finalised, Wilson's table soon attracted press attention as well. Once the commercial interest for the Loopy table was in place, Wilson found a supportive Welsh manufacturer who helped her to work through the construction possibilities until the product was perfect. Available in oak, walnut and maple

AWARDS
Clerkenwell Green
Association Award (2000)
**DTI Export Explorers
Award (2000)**

DESIGN EVENTS
**One Year On,
Business Design Centre,
London (July 1999)**
100% Design, Earls Court,
London (Sept 1999)
**East London Design
Show, Shoreditch Town
Hall, London (Nov 1999)**
Exposition de Design
Britannique, Silvera,
Paris (Jan 2000)

RETAILERS
Aria, London
Harrods, London
Purves & Purves, London

veneers or low-gloss polyurethane finish, this fantastic modern table has already been named an 'antique of the future' by *The Times*, turning the Loopy into an instant design classic.

The understated style that is seen in all of Wilson's products has evolved through an open-minded approach to the way the objects we have in our homes should look, feel and function. Her 'Choob' and 'Millennium Dot' clocks were inspired by a desire to experiment with how we read the time. Neither clock has any fixed numbers, challenging what we expect from a device that is central to the way we plan our lives. Wilson does not look to other furniture for ideas but prefers instead to draw her inspiration from everyday forms. She is wary of too much nostalgia in design and feels it is easy to fall into the

trap of simply rehashing old ideas and design principles. Her main love is discovering new materials and techniques and she plans to begin experimenting with concrete in the near future.

The clean, simple aesthetics of Wilson's pieces, combined with a high level of craftsmanship, should appeal to all those who appreciate quality and durability and while her look is highly contemporary, these are designs that will not date quickly. To produce a table that already has 'classic' status is quite an achievement – watch this space!

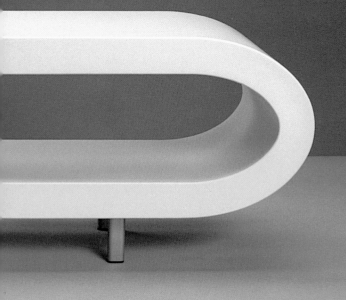

WW.Modcons
Units 2B & 2C
Vanguard Court
36 – 38 Peckham Road
London SE5 8QT
020 7708 4154
07977 035 809

Graduating from the Royal College of Art as a silversmith at the age of 23, William Warren spent a whole year trying to work out how he was going to continue practising his craft in the face of its prohibitive expense. He recalls the moment when he finally hit upon the solution: '…And then all those ideas in silver translated over into stainless steel because I felt I could sell to more people …It was quite a moral issue because I didn't want to sell to only the very rich.' With the simple yet intellectually stimulating 'Negative' range (pictured above), William launched WW.Modcons at Mode: The Contemporary Home Show at the Business Design Centre, Islington, in June 1999.

Although trained in metal, Warren clearly doesn't feel himself limited to that material, as his more recent ranges show. His coffee table made from glass and concrete bollards, the umbrella stand made from a concrete cast of wellington boots (pictured), and the jigsaw-like flooring made from wood are all examples of his willingness to try out new techniques, ideas and materials. For Warren, making a connection with the user and piece is of prime importance.

'It's about connecting people to objects', he told me, 'as soon as you put a bit of personality into something and a bit of thought beyond pure styling …people immediately connect to the object'. Humour is an important device in this respect, as seen, for example, in the darkly wry 'Noose' coat hangers.

Since his launch, Warren has enjoyed considerable success, gathering plenty of press attention that has helped him establish his name. He intends to continue producing accessories and furniture, keeping his creativity alive by remaining flexible in what he takes on, with commissions, domestic interiors, consultancy work and teaching also playing a part in his day-to-day professional life. Showing largely at exhibitions, William is keen to promote his company in the international press. His enthusiasm is truly inspiring, and I look forward to watching his development over the coming years.

THE LIFESTYLE COMPANY ACA
ROUND THE WORLD ALESSI R
ART, FURNITURE & INTERIOR
ARAM DESIGN LTD. DAVID M
LIGNE ROSET CAZ SYSTEMS
APARTMENT STORE LIVING V
OGGETTI AREA SQUARED DE
AERO FALCONER THE LIFESTY
THE NATIONAL TRUST FOR S
THE LONDON LIGHTING CO.
ALMA HOME CHAPLINS OF L
KUME AIMÉ DOMANE INTERIO
DE LA ESPADA FERRIOUS@H

A PURE LIVING WHIPPET MAC
TH ARAM SHOP MISSION IKEA
CARDEN CUNIETTI INHOUSE
LLOR THEMES & VARIATIONS
UBURBIA INDISH WADE SMITH
DUCT ROOST BABYLON ARIA
GN EAT MY HANDBAG BITCH
E COMPANY TANGRAM HEALS
TLAND PLACES AND SPACES
SSEL **DIRECTORY** BOWWOW
NDON LIPP INTERIOR DESIGN
S BOOM! MAKERS CENTURY
ME HABITAT BROWNS LIVING

London North and North West

Acadia
11–13 Essex Road
N1 2SE
020 7354 4464

Ruth Aram Shop
65 Heath Street
NW3 6UG
020 7431 4008

Area Squared Design
357 Upper Street
N1 0PD
020 7278 9689

Aria
295 Upper Street
N1 2TU
020 7704 1999

BOOM!
53 Chalk Farm Road
NW1 8AN
020 7284 4622

Chaplins
477–507 Uxbridge Road
Hatch End, Pinner
Middlesex HA5 4JS
020 8421 1779

Geoffrey Drayton
85 Hampstead Road
NW1 2PL
020 7387 5840

Falconer
362 Muswell Hill Broadway
N10 1DJ
020 8365 3000

Fandango
17 Essex Road
N1 2SE
020 7689 8778

Ikea
2 Drury Way
North Circular Road
NW10 0TH
020 8208 5600
020 8208 5607 for branches nationwide

Indish
13 & 16 Broadway Parade
N8 9DE
020 8340 1144

Living Space
36 Cross Street
N1 2BG
020 7359 3950

London North and North West

Charles Page
61 Fairfax Road
NW6 4EE
020 7328 9851

Planet Bazaar
151 Drummond Street
NW1 2PB
020 7387 8326

twentytwentyone
274 Upper Street
N1 2UA
020 7288 1996

London Central

Alessi
22 Brook Street
W1K 5DF
020 7491 2428

Aram Design
3 Kean Street
WC2B 4AT
020 7240 3933

Browns Living
26 South Molton Street
W1Y 1DA
020 7514 0022

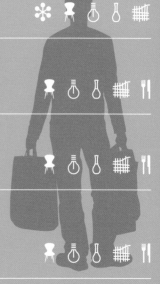

London Central

Century Design
68 Marylebone High Street
W1 3AQ
020 7487 5100

The Conran Collection
12 Conduit Street
W1R 9TG
020 7399 0710

The Conran Shop
55 Marylebone High Street
W1M 3AE
020 7723 2223

Habitat
196 Tottenham Court Road
W1P 9LD
020 7631 3880
0845 60 10 740 for branches nationwide

Heals
196 Tottenham Court Road
W1T 7LQ
020 7636 1666

Noel Hennessy Furniture
6 Cavendish Square
W1G OPD
020 7323 33609

Ligne Roset
23-25 Mortimer Street, W1T 3JE
020 7323 1248

DIRECTORY.LONDON

London Central

Mint
70 Wigmore Street
W1U 2SF
020 7224 4406

Muji
020 7323 2208 for branches nationwide

Purves & Purves
80–81 Tottenham Court Road
W1P 9HD
020 7580 8223

SCP@Selfridges
4th Floor
400 Oxford Street
W1A 1AB
020 7318 3138

Skandium
72 Wigmore Street
W1H 9DL
020 7935 2077

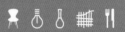

Tom Tom
42 New Compton Street
WC2H 8DA
020 7240 7909

Aero
96 Westbourne Grove
W2 5RT
020 7221 1950

Aimé
32 Ledbury Road
W11 2AB
020 7221 7070

Bowles & Linares
32 Hereford Road
W2 5AJ
020 7229 9886

Bowwow
70 Princedale Road
W11 4NL
020 7792 8532

Carden Cunietti
83 Westbourne Park Road
W2 5QH
020 7229 8630

The Cube
14 Holland Street
W8 4LT
020 7938 2244

London West

Christopher Farr
212 Westbourne Grove
W11 2RH
020 7792 5761

Flow Gallery
1–5 Needham Road
W11 2RP
020 7243 0782

Graham & Green
4, 7 & 10 Elgin Crescent
W11 2JA
020 7727 4594

Isokon Plus
Turnham Green Terrace Mews
W4 1QU
020 8994 0636

Lipp Interior Design
118a Holland Park Avenue
W11 4UA
020 7243 2432

Mission
45 Hereford Road
W2 5AH
020 7792 4633

Ogier
177 Westbourne Grove
W11 2SB
020 7229 0783

London West

Retro Home
20 Pembridge Road
W11 3HL
020 7221 2055

Space
214 Westbourne Grove
W11 2RH
020 7229 6533

Themes & Variations
231 Westbourne Grove
W11 2SE
020 7727 5531

Vessel
114 Kensington Park Road
W11 2PW
020 7727 8001

London South and South West

Aero
347–349 King's Road
SW3 5ES
020 73510511

Babylon Shop
301 Fulham Road
SW10 9QH
020 7376 7255

London South and South West

The Conran Shop
Michelin House
81 Fulham Road
SW3 6RD
020 7589 7401

Designers Guild
267 – 277 King's Road
SW3 5EN
020 7351 5775

De La Espada
60 Sloane Avenue
SW3 3DD
020 7581 4474

Harrods
Knightsbridge
SW1X 7XL
020 7730 1234

The London Lighting Co.
135 Fulham Road
SW3 6RT
020 7589 3612

Makers
40/40a Snowsfield
SE1 3SU
020 7407 7556

David Mellor
4 Sloane Square
SW1W 8EE
020 7730 4259

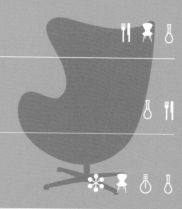

Oggetti
143 Fulham Road
SW3 6SD
020 7581 8088

Places & Spaces
30 Old Town
SW4 OLB
020 7498 0998

Pop UK
17 High Street
SW19 5DX
020 8946 1122

Whippet
190 Upper Richmond Road West
SW14 8AN
020 8878 3141

25 Westow Street
SE19 3RY
020 8771 9493

London East

Alma Home
12–14 Greatorex Street
E1 5NF
020 7377 0762

Nigel Coates
1 Honduras Street
EC1Y OTH
020 7336 1400

Eat My Handbag Bitch
6 Dray Walk
The Old Truman Brewery
E1 6QL
020 7375 3100

Eclectic
202 Brick Lane
E1 6SA
020 7613 3009

Function
1st Floor
12 Greatorex Street
E1 5NF
020 7426 0666

Lifestyle Co.
17 Lamb Street
E1 6EA
020 7247 3503

Mac
142 Clerkenwell Road
EC1R 5DL
020 7713 1234

Overdose on Design
182 Brick Lane
E1 6SP
020 7613 1266

Pure Living
1–3 Leonard Street
EC2A 4AQ
020 7250 1116

SCP
135–139 Curtain Road
EC2A 3BX
020 7739 1869

Viaduct
1–10 Summer's Street
EC1R 5BD
020 7278 8456

Vitra
30 Clerkenwell Road
EC1M 5PQ
020 7608 6200

South

Caz Systems
18–19 Church Street
Brighton
BN1 1RB
01273 326 471

Central
33–35 Little Clarendon Street
Oxford
OX1 2HU
01865 311 141

England at Home
22b Ship Street
Brighton
BN1 1AD
01273 205 544

Kume
20 Bond Street
Brighton
BN1 1RD
01273 602 667

Roost
26 Kensington Gardens
Brighton
BN1 4AL
01273 625 223

South West

Art, Furniture and Interiors
5 Ivor House
Bridge Street
Cardiff
CF1 2TH
0292 040 0800

Shannon
68 Walcot Street
Bath
BA1 5BD
01225 424 222

Suburbia
17 Regent Street
Clifton
Bristol
BS8 4HW
0117 974 3880

Midlands

Atomic
Plumptre Square
Nottingham
NG1 1JF
0115 941 5577

Living
Mechind House
16–17 Lionel Street
Birmingham
B3 1AQ
0121 236 1722

DIRECTORY . AROUND THE UK

Midlands

Luna
23 George Street
Nottingham
NG1 3BH
0115 924 3267

North

Domane Interiors
Union House
5 Bridge Street
Leeds
LS2 7RF
0113 245 0701

The Home
Salts Mill
Victoria Road
Saltaire
Bradford
BD18 3LB
01274 530 770

Loft
24–28 Dock Street
Leeds
LS10 1JF
0113 305 1515

Mason
70 North Street
Leeds
LS2 7PN
0113 242 2434

North

Prego
Arch 17 North Quay
Victoria Quays
Sheffield
S2 5SY
0114 275 5512

North East

Domus
Constance House
117 High Street
Norton, Stockton-on-Tees
TS20 1AA
01642 649 411

North West

Ferrious@Home
Arch 61 Whitworth Street West
Manchester
M1 5WQ
0161 228 6880

Lloyd Davies
14 John Dalton Street
Manchester
M2 6JR
0161 832 3700

North West

Utility
85 Bold Street
Liverpool
L1 4HF
0151 707 9919

Wade Smith Apartment Store
Matthew Street
Liverpool
L2 6RE
0151 224 7617

Scotland

Inhouse
28 Howe Street
Edinburgh
EH3 6TG
0131 225 2888

Inhouse
24 – 26 Wilson Street
Glasgow
G1 1SS
0141 552 5902

The National Trust for Scotland
Hutchesons' Hall
158 Ingram Street
Glasgow
G1 1EJ
0141 552 8391

Scotland

Round The World
15 North West Circus Place
Edinburgh
EH3 6SX
0131 225 7800

Tangram
33/37 Jeffrey Street
Edinburgh
EH1 1DH
0131 556 6551

Kate Wiggin
39 St Stephen Street
Edinburgh
EH3 5AH
0131 225 2606

ACKNOWLEDGMENTS

Author's Acknowledgments

The author would firstly like to thank all of the shop owners, designers, manufacturers, photographers and PR agencies who gave their time and effort to the book. More specifically, he wishes to express his sincere thanks to: Alexei Orlov for all of his kind support and absolute belief throughout this project and for contributing significantly to getting it off the ground; Mazda Cars UK who made this book possible; the Mazda Marketing Team, in particular Clare Wilson who played a key role in the book's progression and who was totally committed at every stage; Steven Yeomans at Mindshare and Simon Speller at The Wow Factory; John Caswell, Ralph Robinson and the team at ROCQM; Caroline Proud, Lorraine Dickey, Leslie Harrington, Bridget Hopkinson, Clare Limpus, Alex Wiltshire and Ellie Hutt at Conran Octopus; and Luke Gifford and Michael Johnson at Johnson Banks.

For their personal encouragement and support, thanks to my parents Anne and John, my sister Annabel, and Lucy, as well as the numerous other friends and relatives who couldn't possibly all be mentioned here.

Publisher's Acknowledgments

Conran Octopus would like to thank all contributing shops, designers and the following manufacturers and photographers for their kind permissions to reproduce their images in this book:

2 Thomas Stewart/Conran Octopus; 10 Thomas Stewart/Conran Octopus; 12 Philip Vile Photography; 14 Patrice Degrandry; 16 Alessi; 18-19 Ed Reeve; 20-21 Aran Design Ltd; 22 Vitra; 24-25 Jonathan Rose; 26 Danica Reklamefolo; 28-29 Fritz Hansen; 30 Vitra; 31 Pete Thompson; 38-39 Warren Dupreez; 40 Francis Amiand; 41 David Loftus; 42-43 Lee Funnell/Graphicphoto; 44 Thomas Stewart/Conran Octopus; 48 Vitra; 50-51 Fritz Hansen; 52-53 Hitch Mylius; 56-57 Rory Carnegie; 60-61 Cloud Nine Photography; 62-63 Ingmar Kurth, Martin URL/e15; 64-65 Guy Drayton Photography; 66-67 Chris Tubbs; 74 Ferrious Ltd; 77 Sam Appleby; 82 Laurence Houghton; 87 Mel Yates; 91 Fritz Hansen; 93 Leonardo Ferrante; 96 -97 Markku Alatalo; 103 Alessi; 107 Enda Bowe; 108-109 Dave Edmonds; 118 B&B Italia; 132 Peter Cook; 134-135 U Schade; 136-137 Graeme Duddridge; 140-141 John Robb Dick; 146-147 Vitra; 164 Peter Barry; 158 Michael Bauke; 162 Knoll International; 164 Maria Satur; 168 Laura Taylor; 169 ChrisTubbs; 170 Pandul Lighting; 174-175 Brenda Burton; 177 Sue Williams; 178-179 B&B Italia; 181 Flash Photodigital; 182-183 Vitra; 185 Robin Day; 192 Miro Zagnoli; 193 Richard Bryant; 197 Lina Ikse Bergman; 208 Ed Reeve; 210 Shot in the Dark; 212 Thomas Stewart; 213 Anthony Dickens; 214-215 Sarah Morris; 219 Tom Elliott; 222-223 Alisdair Smith; 224 A. Jaesckhe; 225 inset Mark Dyson; 230 Colin Hawkins; 238 Thomas Stewart; 240-241 Graeme Duddridge; 244 Julio Garcia Garate; 246-247 Rob Sargent.

The author has made every effort to ensure that the information contained in this book is correct and up to date at time of publication. He apologizes in advance for any unintentional omissions and would be pleased to include up-dated information in subsequent editions.

NOTES

NOTES